A BEGINNER'S GUIDE TO JAPANESE FERMENTATION

Healthy Home-Style Recipes Using Shio Koji, Amazake,
Brown Rice Miso, Nukazuke Pickles & Much More!

Hiroko Shirasaki

TUTTLE Publishing

Tokyo | Rutland, Vermont | Singapore

CONTENTS

Welcome to the World of Japanese Fermentation! 6

The Basics
Old-Fashioned Salty Miso 7
Homemade Shio Koji 8
Amazake, Concentrated Type 10
Homemade Brown Rice Miso 12
White Chickpea Miso 14

Shirasaki's Fermentation Secrets 16

Fermented Foods to Keep on Hand 18

A Few Rules (or Lack of Rules) 20

Clockwise from top: Clams Simmered in Amazake, Clear Soup with Clam Stock, Mitsuba Rice.

PART 1
Spring and Summer Meals

Sautéed Marinated Salmon with Fermented Onion Soup
Fermented Onion Paste 23
Tender Sautéed Salmon with Fermented Onion Sauce 24
Fermented Onion Soup 25
Fermented Onion Salad Dressing 25

Crispy Fried Tuna with Vegetables, Sesame Rice and Miso Soup
Rice with Black Sesame Salt 26
Fried Shio Koji Marinated Tuna Nuggets with Asparagus 27
Radish and Sweet Onion Quick Pickled in Shio Koji 27
Sweet Onion and Radish Leaf Miso Soup 27

Clam Miso Soup with Mixed Grain Rice and Hot Snap Pea Broccoli Salad
Hot Salad of Sugar Snap Peas and Broccoli 28
Clam and White Miso Turmeric Soup 29
Mixed Grain Rice 29
Amazake French Dressing 29

Seafood Steamed in Miso and Wine with Watercress Rice and Crudités
Sea Bream and Clams Steamed in White Miso and Wine 31
Watercress Rice 31
White Miso Lemon Dip Crudités 31

Rice Bran Pickles and Natto Fritters

Easy Rice Bran Pickles (Nukazuke) 33
Delicious Natto and Green Bean Fritters 34
Mountain Yam White Miso Soup 35
Mixed "Black" Rice 35

Clams Simmered in Amazake with Mitsuba Rice and Clam Stock with Tofu

Clam Stock with Tofu 36
Clams Simmered in Amazake 37
Mitsuba Rice 37

Mackerel and Amazake Curry with Iced Lemon Lassi

Mackerel and Amazake Curry 39
Amazake Lemon Lassi Drink 39

Seafood Soy Milk Yogurt Curry with Lemon Rice and Yogurt Marinated Cabbage

Homemade Soy Milk Yogurt 41
Seafood and Soy Milk Yogurt Curry 42
Red Cabbage Marinated in Yogurt 43
Lemon Rice 43

Kimchi and Tofu Rice Bowl with Vegetable Miso Soup

Homemade Cabbage Amazake Kimchi 45
Spring Vegetable Miso Soup 45
Kimchi and Tofu Rice Bowl 45

Mirin Pickles with Amazake Fruit Yogurt

Amazake Fruit Yogurt 46
Homemade Mirin Pickles 47
Pickled Beans, Burdock Root and Mushrooms 47
Pickled Bell Pepper and Onion 47
Pickled Bean Tapanade 47

Plum Miso Octopus with Ginger Rice, Kudzu Tofu and Zucchini Miso Soup

Refreshing Plum or Apricot Miso 49
White Sesame Kudzu Tofu 50
Octopus and Cucumber with Plum Miso 51
Zucchini and Aburaage Miso Soup 51
Ginger Rice 51

Mackerel and Amazake Curry

Soba with Green Chili Miso and Eggplant Sautéed in Ume Vinegar

Fragrant Green Chili Miso 53

Green Chili Miso, Spinach and Natto Soba Noodles 54

Eggplant Sautéed in Ume Vinegar 55

Mixed Vegetable Sushi Rice and Tofu Topped with Fermented Ginger

Sushi Rice with Fermented Ginger and Mixed Vegetables 57

Tofu Topped with Fermented Ginger 57

Fermented Myoga Ginger and Regular Ginger 57

Sea Bream and Pickled Daikon Sushi with Clear Broccolini Soup

Crunchy Dried Daikon Pickled with Amazake 59

Sea Bream and Pickled Daikon Sushi 60

Clear Soup with Broccolini 61

Sea Bream and Pickled Daikon Sushi, Clear Soup with Broccolini

PART 2

Fall and Winter Meals

Tofu and Shiitake Bibimbap with Korean Style Vegetables and Leek Soup

Homemade Amazake Gochujang 65

Tofu and Shiitake Mushroom Bibimbap 66

White Leek Soup 66

Four Types of Namul 67

Root Vegetable Miso Soup with Millet Rice and Miso Pickles

Root Vegetable Soup with Miso 69

Diced Vegetables Pickled in Miso 69

Glutinous Millet Rice 69

Panfried Fish and Vegetables Marinated in Sake Lees with Bean Sprout Soup

Sake Lees Pickling Base (Kasudoko) 71

Panfried Fish Marinated in Sake Lees 72

Vegetables Pickled in Sake Lees 73

Bean Sprout and Sake Lees Soup 73

Creamy Oysters Sautéed in Sake Lees and Soy Milk with Peppers Marinated in Ume Vinegar

Sake Lees Paste 75

Creamy Oysters Sautéed in Sake Lees and Soy Milk 77

Bell Peppers Marinated in Ume Vinegar 77

Mushroom and Oyster Turmeric Rice with Marinated Mushrooms and Vegetable Mushroom Soup

Mushrooms Marinated in Shio Koji 79
Mushroom and Oyster Turmeric Rice 80
Mushroom Vegetable Soup 81
Greens with Marinated Mushrooms 81

Stir-Fried Pickled Greens with Millet Rice, Natto and Mackerel and Daikon Sake Lees Soup

Salted Pickled Greens 83
Stir-Fried Pickled Greens 85
Mackerel and Daikon Sake Lees Soup 85

Panfried Swordfish with Spicy Miso, Cucumber Salad, Okra Miso Soup and Barley Rice

Spicy Miso Sauce 87
Panfried Swordfish with Lettuce Leaves and Spicy Miso 88
Barley Rice 88
Cucumber Salad 89
Spicy Okra Miso Soup 89

Mackerel Simmered in Sake with Pickled Greens, Sweet Potato Rice and Root Vegetable Soy Milk Miso Soup

Greens Pickled in Rice Bran 90
Mackerel Simmered in Sake and Fermented Rice Bran 91
Daikon and Carrot Miso Soy Milk Soup 91
Sweet Potato Rice 91

Tempeh Teriyaki with Brown Rice and Umeboshi Seaweed Soup

Homemade Fermented Mayonnaise 93
Tempeh Teriyaki 94
Umeboshi and Kombu Seaweed Soup 95

Tofu Cheese Salad with Creamy Kabocha Soy Milk Soup

Tofu Cheese Salad 96
Shio Koji Tofu Cheese 97
Creamy Kabocha Soy Milk Soup 97

Shio Koji Potatoes Gratin with Vegetable Lentil Soup and Quick Pickles

Shio Koji White Sauce 99
Shio Koji Potatoes Gratin 100
Red Cabbage and Radish Quick Pickles 101
Lentil and Napa Cabbage Shio Koji Tomato Soup 101

Salmon and Napa Cabbage with Fermented Aromatic Chili Oil

Salmon and Napa Cabbage Hot Pot 103
Fermented Aromatic Chili Oil 103

Recipe Index by Ingredient 104
Your Fermentation Pantry 108
Fermented Foods Are All You Need! 111

Welcome to the World of Japanese Fermentation!

Many people assume that fermented foods are difficult to make, but they couldn't be more wrong. Using a few tried-and-true shortcuts, you can prepare a range of healthy superfoods that in the end will save you time. Many of the foods keep in the fridge for a long time, so make a batch to have on hand. As the fermentation process continues, the flavors change, growing deeper and more complex.

What about store-bought fermented foods and ingredients? Sure, it's always an option to pick up commercially produced miso, shio koji and amazake, but using my easy techniques, you'll soon prefer you own home-made concoctions. They typically taste better and the nutritional benefits

Fermented foods can play a range of roles—both starring and support-ing—in your daily diet. The benefits are manifold. Your dishes and meals will not only brim with taste and flavor, but it's the long-term health benefits that will keep you coming back for more. Key to maintaining gut health, the high-performing probiotics and mighty microbes of fermented foods are the essential elements for internal balance and better digestion.

Using simple ingredients and easy-to-follow preparation methods, you can quickly create complex flavor profiles and unleash the nutritive power of fermented foods. The sample menus included here are just the beginning. Soon you'll be adapting your own recipes, substituting your healthy D.I.Y. ferments in new and surprisingly tasty ways.

—Hiroko Shirasaki

The Basics

Old-Fashioned Salty Miso

Miso prepared four years ago. It's turned a little dark.

There are many forms of miso, each has its own merits and particular uses. But if I had to choose my personal favorite, classic salty miso would be my go-to option every time.

Among at-home fermenters, sweet miso is certainly growing in popularity. It typically contains more rice koji than beans. Or you can simply mix in a generous portion of amazake to turn old-fashioned salty miso into its sweeter alter ego. In smaller doses, amazake offsets the saltiness of traditional miso, balancing it while also adding a pleasing complexity to the flavors it imparts.

Long-lasting, resistant to mold or rapid spoilage, miso is high in protein and brings a new flexibility and freedom to some of the traditional dishes you love. Onigiri (or rice balls) coated in salty miso are delicious! Unlike the ones made with koji-based miso, this version doesn't become watery and the rice doesn't get dry.

This fantastic ferment also keeps in the fridge for a long time. Miso that has turned dark over time is delicious in a stir-fry or stirred into a sauce. Even more magical, you can use the leftovers as a starter for the next batch. Just add a little bit to the new preparation to kick-start the fermentation process and to keep the miso mold-free.

To make salty miso, the ratio of rice koji to beans is 1:1, and sea salt is half the ratio of beans. In other words, ½ cup (100 g) of beans requires ½ cup (100 g) of koji and 2¾ tablespoons (50 g) of sea salt.

Homemade Shio Koji

Shio koji intensifies the flavor of any ingredient, a power pairing that makes your dishes even more delicious!

Shio koji is gaining in popularity as a substitute seasoning that enhances flavor and taste in place of salt. It requires only salt and dried rice koji to produce, so why not try my favorite preparation and whip up a quick batch of this versatile seasoning? If you have a simple yogurt maker, you can set some going before you head to bed. Come morning, you'll have the a thick, slightly sweet shio koji ready to power pack your favorite foods.

If you're preparing shio koji at room temperature, the key is to add water to keep the koji from drying out. After it's been stored for several days, the water will evaporate, so be sure to keep your developing ferment well-hydrated.

Shio koji can be used in a variety of tasty ways. Whether with vegetables, meat or fish, mixing or marinating your chosen ingredients quickly in shio koji will lift the level of their flavors. Use it as a seasoning for fried chicken or a base for quick pickles. Add it to your favorite soup or to a béchamel sauce for gratin. The recipes and ideas presented in here are just the beginning.

Shelf life: 1 MONTH IN THE REFRIGERATOR

1 cup (200 g) dried rice koji
1¼ cups (300 ml) water
4 tablespoons (70 g) sea salt

NOTE Dried rice koji is easy to obtain year-round from Asian or Japanese markets, health food stores and online. If you're able to find fresh rice koji, use a little less water for this recipe.

Instructions

Crumble the dried rice koji, separating it with your hands, then place it into a clean preserving container and add the salt.

Add the water, mix well and let stand at room temperature.

Mix it well once a day. Add more water if the mixture dries out. It's ready at room temperature in about a week in the summer and after two weeks in the winter.

If you have a yogurt maker, you can make shio koji by combining all the ingredients in a container and maintaining the temperature at 140°F (60°C) for 6 hours without adding water.

Amazake, Concentrated Type

Amazake fuses the natural sweetness of rice with the tangy pop of umami to impart new depths of fermented flavor to your dishes.

There are two main types of amazake: white rice and brown rice. The version made from white rice is milder and suitable for making desserts and sweets, while richly flavored brown-rice amazake is useful for general cooking. To make this thick and smooth seasoning, all you need is a yogurt maker to produce the concentrated form of amazake used as the basis for many of the recipes included here.

If you don't have a yogurt maker, simply boil rice and water in a heavy saucepan, cool it to 140°F (60°C), then stir in the rice koji. Remove the pan from the heat, wrap it in a towel to keep it warm and occasionally put it back on low heat to maintain a consistent low-graade temperature. When it's ready, it can be pureed in a blender to produce this smooth and slightly sweet seasoning. If you want prefer your amazake in beverage form, just mix 1 part amazake to 2 parts water or carbonated water and enjoy!

Shelf life: 2 WEEKS IN THE REFRIGERATOR

1 cup (200 g) dried rice koji
1 cup (200 g) cooked white Japanese rice, semi-polished rice or brown rice
¾ cup (200 ml) water

NOTE You can use brown rice koji instead of regular white rice koji in this recipe.

Instructions

1 Put all the ingredients in a yogurt maker. If the rice is freshly cooked, cool it to room temperature first. Cold rice can be used as is.

2 Shake the container well to mix. Turn the container upside down or sideways to mix it thoroughly.

3 Set the container in the yogurt maker, and leave at 140°F (60°C) for 6 hours.

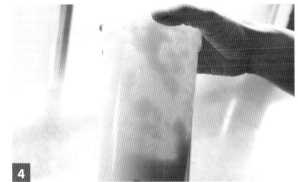

4 Remove the container from time to time, open the lid to release the pressure, replace and tighten the lid again and give it a good shake to mash the rice koji and make the amazake smooth.

Homemade Brown Rice Miso

All you need is a plastic bag to create the delicious homemade texture of brown rice miso.

Have you ever made miso by hand? Prepaing a large batch can be daunting, but with my simple approach and time-saving shortcuts, it's never been easier.

All you need are beans, salt and rice koji, that's it. And that plastic bag I mentioned. The brown rice yields a richer more flavorful miso than its milder, white-rice-based counterpart.

If you use soybeans, the miso will be heavy and sticky, while chickpeas will create a melt-in-your-mouth texture similar to a silky bean paste. After boiling and mashing the beans, mix them thoroughly with rice koji and salt, add the boiling water. It may take a long time to cook, but you'll be surprised at the delicious taste of the first bite.

The recipe makes 1 lb, 2 oz (500 g), which is about the same as a packet of store-bought miso. But who needs commercially produced products when my at-home version yields even tastier and healthier results?

Makes 1 lb 2 oz or 500 g miso
Shelf life: 1 YEAR IN THE REFRIGERATOR

½ cup (100 g) dried soybeans or chickpeas
3 tablespoons (50 g) sea salt
¾ cup (150 g) dried brown rice koji

NOTE You can also use regular white rice koji to make a milder white miso.

Instructions

1 Soak the soybeans or chickpeas for a full day in water in a pot. Drain, put in fresh water and boil until tender. (Reserve the cooking liquid.)

2 Put the beans in a plastic bag white still hot and mash them up using the bottom of a glass or other implement (to about the consistency of mashed potatoes).

3 Put the dried rice koji and salt in another plastic bag, fill the bag with air, twist the top and shake well to mix while holding the top shut.

4 When the rice koji is evenly coated with salt, it's ready.

5 Put the mashed beans in the plastic bag containing the rice koji and salt.

6 Add enough of the bean cooking liquid from Step 1 to bring the weight up to 1 lb 2 oz (500 g).

7 Knead the bag well to distribute and combine all the ingredients evenly. Push all the air out of the bag and close it up. Leave at room temperature for about 3 months.

8 Open the bag occasionally, knead the contents, push out the air again and close up the bag. It's even better if you wrap the bag tightly in a piece of cloth or kitchen towel.

9 Taste the miso periodically and when it has fermented as much as you like, transfer the miso to a storage container and refrigerate.

White Chickpea Miso

Mild, sweet, versatile and quicker to make!

The great thing about white miso is that you can really taste the sweetness of the rice koji. It doesn't need to ferment as much, so it no longer tastes like "shio koji with beans." And you don't have to wait as long to eat it, so it's ideal for people who are making miso for the first time.

Using white rice koji instead of brown rice koji reduces the pungent aroma of the miso and lightens its color. You can also make delicious miso us-

ing white beans instead of soybeans or chickpeas.

If you have a yogurt maker, you can make it at 140°F (60°C) in just 8 hours, no time at all.

Since it's low in salt and doesn't have as much of the pungent fermented taste of regular miso, you can use it in lots of different ways. Besides using it in miso soup, you can make spicy soups, vegetable dips or use it as a marinade for fish or chicken.

Makes 1 lb 4 oz or 550 g miso
Shelf life: **3 MONTHS IN THE REFRIGERATOR**

½ cup (100 g) dried soybeans or chickpeas (or white beans)
2 tablespoons (35 g) salt
1 cup (200 g) dried white rice koji

NOTE If you want to make it smoother, add the rice koji, salt and lukewarm water at Step 3 and blend the mixture in a food processor.

Instructions

1
Soak the chickpeas for a full day in water in a pot. Drain, put in fresh water, and boil until tender. (Reserve the cooking liquid.)

2
Drain the chickpeas in a colander, and roll them between your fingers to remove the skins. They will come off easily. Discard the skins.

3
Place the peeled chickpeas in a plastic bag while they are still warm and mash with the bottom of a glass or a similar implement (to about the consistency of mashed potatoes).

4
Put the rice koji and salt in another plastic bag, fill the bag with air and shake well to mix.

5
Place the mashed chickpeas in the Step 4 bag.

6
Add enough of the warm cooking liquid from Step 1 to bring the total weight up to 1 lb 4 oz (550 g).

7
Knead the bag well to combine the contents well. Push all the air out of the bag and close it up. Leave at room temperature for a week in the spring and summer, or for 3 weeks in the winter.

8
Open up the bag occasionally, knead the contents well, push out the air again and close up the bag. It is even better if you wrap the bag tightly in a piece of cloth or kitchen towel.

9
Taste the miso periodically and when it has fermented as much as you like, transfer the miso to a storage container and refrigerate.

Shirasaki's Fermentation Secrets

They Keep for a Long Time

Fermented foods were embraced in Japan as a form of preservation when refrigeration was not an option. Fermentation suppresses the growth of bacteria and enhances the preservation of foods. In addition, koji, natto (fermented soybeans), lactic acid bacteria and other fermented ingredients have sterilizing effects.

Foods Become Tastier as They Mature!

In addition to enhancing preservation, the fermentation process allows the food to mature over time. The enzymes contained in the ingredients enhance the taste, and the decomposition and fermentation of sugars and proteins create a unique flavor profile. The appeal of fermentation is that it doesn't require a lot of work to yield a delicious result.

Gut Health

As you already know with the case of yogurt, some of the bacterias found in fermented foods do the body good. While many love these fiesty ferments for the flavors they impart, there's a considerable cohort that turns to these foods for the intestinal balance and gut health they promote and improve.

The Softer Side

It's common knowledge that the active enzymes in fermented food help break down proteins. Fermented Onion Paste (page 23), for example, enhances the flavor and helps it keep longer.

Added Sugar Isn't Needed

Sugar is often used in cooking to add depth of flavor and a sweet or salty taste. In this book, the natural sweetness and richness of amazake is the main ingredient used to expand the flavors of recipes. These recipes are also suitable for those who are concerned about consuming too much sugar for health or general dietary reasons.

Fermented Foods to Keep on Hand

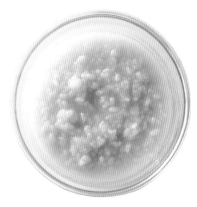

Shio Koji

A traditional fermented flavor enhancer

Shio koji is an all-purpose seasoning made from salt and fermented rice. It brings out the true flavor of ingredients in any dish. It's also a versatile product, useful for seasoning meat and fish, simmered dishes, sauces, dressings and more. It can be used in place of salt or soy sauce in all kinds of dishes. See page 9 for a homemade recipe.

Amazake

Can be used in place of sugar!

Amazake is a traditional sweet drink in Japan made from fermented rice. It is low or no-alcohol. It tastes great on its own, but it's also useful in daily preparations. Its thickening properties, umami and sweetness make it a good base for curries, sauces, marinades and soups. This book uses a concentrated type that lasts for a long time. Note that this version of amazake is not a light drink. See page 11 for a homemade recipe.

Pickles

The longer you let them sit, the better they taste!

There are various types of pickles, such as the standard nukazuke (rice bran pickles), kasuzuke (sake lees pickles), miso pickles and brine or vinegar pickles. They're useful for cooking because of the health benefits of their minerals and lactic acid bacteria, as well as the umami they impart. See pages 27, 33, 47, 59, 69, 73, 83, 90, and 101 for a variety of different pickles you can make at home.

Miso

The flavor of soybeans and sweetness of rice koji combined

Miso is one of the basic seasonings found in every home in Japan and is widely available elsewhere. If you can choose one version that suits your tastes or make your own, your fermentation world will dramatically expand. The taste of miso varies depending on the type of beans used and the degree of maturity. You can rely on miso for all your cooking needs, no matter what type of cuisine you are preparing. See pages 7 and 10–15 for homemade recipes.

Natto

Known as an acquired taste; try a number of different brands to find one you like

Natto is a variety of fermented soybeans rich in natto bacillus. The natto bacillus breaks down the protein in soybeans and increases the amount of amino acids, resulting in a delicious fresh fermentation product. I recommend using natto made from Japanese soybeans and produced in the traditional way. The sticky consistency of natto takes some getting used to, but once you get beyond that to appreciate the rich flavor, you may find it addictive! It has tremendous health benefits also.

Soy Milk Yogurt

A basic fermented food you'll want to eat every day!

This yogurt is made by fermenting soy milk. See page 41 for a homemade recipe. It's an essential ingredient in dishes that require a creamy, mild flavor without the use of dairy products. It's rich in vegetable protein and isoflavones. It can of course be substituted with regular yogurt.

A Few Rules (or Lack of Rules)

You can easily make basic fermented ingredients at home. Or you can buy them pre-made at your local market or specialty store. The freshly made versions generally have more nutritional content. Most fermented foods can keep in the fridge for several weeks or longer. So you can take full advantage of their versatility, adding them to your favorite dishes while trying new ones!

▧ 1 tablespoon is 15 milliliters, 1 teaspoon is 5 milliliters, and 1 cup is 240 milliliters. All ingredients are measured by leveling.

▧ Unless noted otherwise, soy sauce means regular soy sauce, salt means sea salt (made with 100% seawater), and vinegar means rice vinegar. You can also use wine vinegar, but dilute it with water to reduce the sourness.

▧ The salt content of commercially available miso, shio koji and soy sauce products varies, so adjust the recipes accordingly to taste.

▧ Some processes, such as vegetable washing and peeling, are omitted.

▧ Frying pans used here are made of iron and pots are made of stainless steel. The material and thickness of the pan will affect the heating and cooking time, so please use the indicated numbers as a guide.

▧ The shelf lives of fermented ingredient recipes are approximate. They'll vary depending on the ingredients used and the season and climate, so be sure to taste the foods before adding them to recipes.

PART 1

Spring and Summer Meals

This is the time of year when temperatures are rising and we want to eat something light and refreshing. Take advantage of the flexibility of fermentation by pairing it with plenty of seasonal vegetables. As long as you have a stock of fermented items, you can prepare your meals in no time! Here are some recipes that can be used as main dishes, side dishes or soups and starters. They're perfect for daily dinners as well as weekend breakfasts and lunches.

Sautéed Marinated Salmon with Fermented Onion Soup

Fermented Onion Salad Dressing ➡ Page 25

Fermented Onion Soup ➡ Page 25

Tender Sautéed Salmon with Fermented Onion Sauce ➡ Page 24

Fermented Onion Paste

If you have this versatile three-ingredient paste on hand, it can be used as a marinade, in a soup or as a dressing. Or discover some new and flavorful uses: it's up to you!

Fermented Onion Paste

Cod, swordfish, chicken breast—in other words, any proteins that tend to be on the dry side—can be made juicy and moist just by marinating them in this paste. If made with sweet onions, it tastes fresh and delicious!

Shelf life: 1 WEEK IN THE REFRIGERATOR

1 large onion (7 oz/200 g)
½ cup (100 g) Homemade Shio Koji (see page 9 for a homemade recipe)
2 teaspoons rice vinegar

NOTES The vinegar takes away the pungency of the onion and makes the paste easy to store. It can be made in a blender or processor in batches without grating the onion. Puree it until you've achieved the desired consistency.

Instructions

1 Grate the onion (or you can purée it in a blender or food processor.)

2 Put all the ingredients in a bowl and mix well. Keep in a sealed jar in the refrigerator until used.

Uses for Fermented Onion Paste

➡ IN CURRY
Meat or fish can be marinated in the paste, and then the whole thing can be simmered, paste and all. Even if you don't have a thickening roux, oil and curry powder are all you need to make a refreshing and healthy curry.

➡ DELICIOUS IN POTATO SALAD
While the boiled potatoes are still hot, mash them with the onion paste. Add mayonnaise and mix with ingredients to create a potato salad that tastes like it came from a great deli.

➡ AS AN INSTANT SOUP BASE
Just add 1 tablespoon of the onion paste to ¾ cup (200 ml) water or kombu seaweed water and bring to a boil to make a soup for one. Add other ingredients to the soup if you like.

Tender Sautéed Salmon with Fermented Onion Sauce

The aroma of fermented onions and garlic makes this an appetizing main dish. Simple grilled fish is elevated just by marinating it.

Serves 2

¾ lb (300 g) salmon filets

MARINADE
4 tablespoons (65 g) Fermented
   Onion Paste (see page 23)
1 tablespoon olive oil
1 garlic clove, sliced

1 Mix the Marinade together in a shallow container, spread on the salmon filets and leave to marinate for at least 15 minutes.
2 Put the salmon filets with the paste in a cold frying pan, and panfry the salmon slowly over low-medium heat on both sides until cooked, then remove them to a plate.
3 Reduce the sauce that is left in the pan a little and pour over the salmon. Serve with sautéed vegetables on the side.

NOTE The salmon can be left to marinate in the refrigerator overnight or longer to make it even more moist and succulent.

Fermented Onion Soup

Serves 2

4 tablespoons (65 g) Fermented
  Onion Paste (see page 23)
1 large potato
6 to 8 cherry tomatoes
2 to 3 broccoli florets
1⅔ cups (400 ml) water
One 2-inch (5-cm) square piece
  dried kombu seaweed
Salt and pepper, to taste

1 Cut the potato into bite-sized pieces, coat with the onion paste and leave to marinate for 5 minutes.
2 Put the potatoes and water in a pot, break up the kombu seaweed and add that as well. Heat over medium. When it comes to a boil, skim the surface, turn the heat down to low and simmer for 10 to 15 minutes until the potato is tender.
3 Add the cherry tomatoes and broccoli, and simmer for an additional 5 minutes or so. Taste and adjust the seasoning with salt and pepper.

NOTE If you add ½ of a bay leaf to the kombu seaweed, the soup will taste like a refined consommé.

Fermented Onion Salad Dressing

3 tablespoons (50 g) Fermented Onion Paste (see page 23)
1 tablespoon lemon juice
1 tablespoon vegetable oil

Mix all the ingredients together well. Pour over lettuce or microgreens.

Crispy Fried Tuna with Vegetables, Sesame Rice and Miso Soup

Fried Shio Koji Marinated Tuna Nuggets with Asparagus

Radish and Sweet Onion Quick Pickled in Shio Koji

Rice with Black Sesame Salt

Sweet Onion and Radish Leaf Miso Soup

With shio koji, which can be easily used in place of salt, fried foods can be seasoned in a single shot, bringing out the flavor of the individual ingredients.

Rice with Black Sesame Salt

2 servings cooked white or brown rice, about 2 cups (400 g)
1 tablespoon black sesame seeds
1 teaspoon salt

Put the sesame seeds and salt in a frying pan and toast over very low heat. When a couple of the sesame seeds pop, remove immediately. Leave to cool, and sprinkle on top of the rice.

Fried Shio Koji Marinated Tuna Nuggets with Asparagus

Serves 2

½ lb (225 g) fresh tuna
6 asparagus stalks
¼ cup (50 g) Homemade Shio Koji (see page 9 for a homemade recipe)
1 garlic clove
One 2-inch (5-cm) piece ginger
Cornstarch or potato starch
Oil, for deep frying
1 lemon wedge, for serving

1 Grate the garlic and ginger. Cut the asparagus into easy-to-eat pieces, and cut the tuna into bite-sized pieces.
2 Put the garlic, ginger, shio koji and tuna into a plastic bag and rub the seasonings into the fish. Refrigerate for at least 30 minutes, up to overnight.
3 Put some cornstarch in a separate plastic bag and add the tuna pieces. Toss to coat them evenly.
4 Heat some oil for deep frying to 340–360°F (170–180°C) and quickly deep fry the asparagus. Next, deep fry the skipjack tuna from Step 3 until crispy and golden brown. Serve with the lemon wedge.

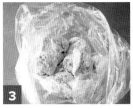

Radish and Sweet Onion Quick Pickled in Shio Koji

Serves 2

10 radishes
¼ sweet onion
(Alternatively you can use ½ lb/200 g) of mixed vegetables, cubed)
4 teaspoons (25 g) Homemade Shio Koji (see page 9 for a homemade recipe)
1 teaspoon rice vinegar

1 Cut the radishes in half. Cut the onion into smaller pieces than the radish pieces.
2 Put all the ingredients in a plastic bag and rub the vegetables to coat well with the shio koji and rice vinegar. Leave to marinate for about 30 minutes.

Sweet Onion and Radish Leaf Miso Soup

Serves 2

1 sweet onion
Radish leaves from a small bunch
1¼ cups (300 ml) kombu seaweed water (see page 35)
2 tablespoons (35 g) miso (see pages 12–15 for homemade recipes)
A pinch of salt

1 Chop up the sweet onion and the radish leaves roughly.
2 Put the kombu seaweed water and the onion in a pan, add the salt and heat over low. When it comes to a boil, simmer for about 10 minutes until the onion is tender. Add the radish leaves. Dissolve the miso in some of the cooking liquid in a separate small bowl or in the ladle, then add to the soup.

Clam Miso Soup with Mixed Grain Rice and Hot Snap Pea Broccoli Salad

Hot Salad of Sugar Snap Peas and Broccoli

Mixed Grain Rice

Clam and White Miso Turmeric Soup

The soup combines the sweetness and umami of clam broth with the subtly tangy punch of white miso. A simple preparation, it's just poured over the rice.

Hot Salad of Sugar Snap Peas and Broccoli

Serves 2

2 broccoli florets
5 sugar snap peas
2 tablespoons (35 g) Amazake French Dressing (see page 29)

Remove the strings from the sugar snap peas and cut in half. Cut the broccoli up into small pieces. Blanch both briefly, about 2 minutes, drain well and mix with the dressing while still hot.

Clam and White Miso Turmeric Soup

Serves 2

¾ lb (350 g) Manila or littleneck clams (see page 37 for the cleaning procedure)
1 medium onion
2 tablespoons white miso (35 g) (see page 15 for a homemade recipe)
Scant ½ cup (100 ml) unsweetened soy milk
1¼ cups (300 ml) water
½ teaspoon turmeric powder
Salt and pepper, to taste
1½ tablespoons vegetable oil
Mixed grain rice, cooked, to serve
Watercress, to serve
Lemon wedges, to serve

1 Add the oil, chopped onion and garlic to a pan and sauté over low heat until the onion is softened. Add the turmeric and sauté a minute more.
2 Add ⅓ of the water and the clams and cover the pan. When the clams open up, remove the clams from about half the shells. Discard the shells and returns the clams to the broth.
3 Add the rest of the water. When it comes to a boil, skim the surface.
4 Add the white miso and soy milk and heat through. Season with salt and pepper. Put some mixed grain rice in a bowl and ladle the soup over it. Eat topped with watercress and lemon.

NOTE Don't be stingy with the seasoning here!

Mixed Grain Rice

Serves 2

1 cup (150 g) uncooked rice
2 tablespoons mixed grains such as barley or millet
A pinch of sea salt

1 Rinse the rice and place in a pot with ¾ cup (200 ml) water. Put the mixed grains in a small bowl and cover with plenty of water. Leave both to soak for at least 30 minutes.
2 Drain the mixed grains well and add to the rice with a pinch of salt. Mix once, cover the pan and heat over high until the water comes to a boil. Turn the heat down as low as possible, and cook for 15 minutes. Raise the heat to high again for a few seconds until you hear crackling sounds coming from the pan. Take the pan off the heat and leave the rice to steam and rest for 15 minutes.

NOTE The rice should be on the firm side (al dente) to go with the soup.

Amazake French Dressing

Serves 2
Shelf life: 1 WEEK IN THE REFRIGERATOR

A INGREDIENTS
2 tablespoons amazake, concentrated type (see page 11 for a homemade recipe)
2 tablespoons rice vinegar
1 teaspoon sea salt
⅓ teaspoon grated garlic
A pinch of white pepper

2 tablespoons vegetable oil

1 Put the **A** ingredients in a bowl and mix well with a whisk to dissolve the salt.
2 Add the oil little by little and mix in one direction until emulsified.

Seafood Steamed in Miso and Wine with Watercress Rice and Crudités

Watercress Rice

White Miso Lemon Dip Crudités

Sea Bream and Clams Steamed in White Miso and Wine

Steam some miso-marinated fish in white wine for a feast in the style of an Italian acqua pazza! The crunchy raw vegetables and silky lemon-flavored dip are the perfect starter.

Sea Bream and Clams Steamed in White Miso and Wine

Serves 2

½ lb (250 g) sea bream, seabass or mackerel
1½ tablespoons (25 g) white miso (see page 15 for a homemade recipe)
⅓ lb (150 g) rinsed and scrubbed Manila or littleneck clams (see page 37 for the cleaning procedure)
½ medium onion
8 to 10 cherry tomatoes
3 to 4 sugar snap peas
2 garlic cloves
1½ tablespoons olive oil
Scant ½ cup (100 ml) white wine
Salt and pepper, to taste
Watercress, to serve

NOTE
• You can use 1 scant tablespoon of shio koji instead of the miso.
• When spreading the miso on the fish pieces, you can also put them in a plastic bag and give them a few gentle shakes.

1 Sprinkle the fish pieces with a little salt and pepper and then spread the miso on both sides. Refrigerate for at least 30 minutes or overnight. Slice the onion thinly. Remove the strings from the sugar snap peas and cut in half. Finely mince the garlic cloves.
2 Heat the olive oil over low heat in a frying pan. Put in the fish pieces skin side down and panfry until golden brown. Turn and repeat on the other side.
3 Add the garlic, clams, sweet onion, cherry tomatoes and white wine, cover the pan and cook over medium heat until it comes to a boil. Add the sugar snap peas, turn the heat down low and cook until the clams open up. Adjust the seasoning with salt and pepper, and serve with some watercress on the side, if desired.

Watercress Rice

Serves 2

2 servings cooked white or brown rice (2 cups/400 g)
1 bunch watercress
2 pinches of sea salt, plus more to taste
Olive oil, to taste

Finely chop the watercress and sprinkle with salt. When the moisture drains out, squeeze the pieces lightly. Mix with the olive oil into the rice, and adjust the seasoning with a little more salt.

White Miso Lemon Dip Crudités

Serves 2

2 tablespoons (35 g) white miso (see page 15 for a homemade recipe)
1 tablespoon olive oil
1½ teaspoons lemon juice
Cabbage leaves, carrot sticks, celery stalks and cucumber sticks, to serve

Mix all the ingredients together. Serve with spring cabbage, carrot sticks, celery stalks or cucumber sticks.

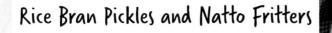

Rice Bran Pickles and Natto Fritters

Easy Rice Bran Pickles (Nukazuke)

Mountain Yam White Miso Soup ➡ Page 35

Delicious Natto and Green
Bean Fritters ➡ Page 34

Mixed "Black" Rice ➡ Page 35

This healthy and highly satisfying rice-based meal combines
crispy natto kakiage with brightly colored rice bran pickles.

Easy Rice Bran Pickles (Nukazuke)

This is a great introduction to fermentation pickling! This bed of fermented rice bran takes a little time to develop, but it can be used to pickle multiple batches of vegetables. You don't have to mix it every day; just keep it in the refrigerator on warm days or when you're busy. Use any kinds of vegetables you like and pickle them in the rice bran at your leisure.

4¼ cups (500 g) fresh rice bran, or lightly moistened dry rice bran
2 cups plus 1 tablespoon (500 ml) water
3 tablespoons (50 g) sea salt
2 to 3 small potatoes
1 lb (500 g) vegetables of your choice (pickling cucumbers,
    baby carrots, potatoes, radishes, etc.)

Instructions

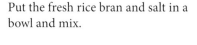

1
Put the fresh rice bran and salt in a bowl and mix.

2
Make a well in the middle of the rice bran, pour in the water and mix well.

3
Transfer the mixture to a non-reactive container, and start by pickling the peeled and thickly sliced potatoes. (This will start the pickling bed fermentation.)

4
After one day, take the sliced vegetables out, squeeze their juices into the pickling bed (vegetables are delicious shredded and stir-fried with a bit of garlic), and mix up the pickling bed.

5
Rub the other vegetables you are pickling with a little salt, then after about 10–15 minutes squeeze out the excess moisture.

6
Smooth the surface of the pickling bed, push the vegetables in, and cover them with the pickling bed mixture. Pickle the vegetables for half a day to a whole day.

NOTES
• Avoid putting onions or garlic in the pickling bed until the fermentation process is complete. When water comes out of the bed, press it down and let the water drain out by using a small cup or other object with a flat bottom.
• The sliced vegetables removed in Step 4 are delicious if they are soaked in water for a bit, shredded, and stir-fried with garlic.
• If more rice bran is needed, add 10% of the existing amount of bran and salt, mix well, and let sit for a few days to ferment.
• You can use any leftover fermented rice bran in the recipe on page 91, Mackerel Simmered in Sake and Fermented Rice Bran.

Delicious Natto and Green Bean Fritters

When fried, the peculiar taste and odor of natto disappear and the texture becomes light and fluffy!

Serves 2

2 packets natto (3 oz/90 g)
½ cup (50 g) green beans or other
   vegetables of your choice
Vegetable oil, for deep frying
Grated ginger, to serve
Soy sauce, to serve

BATTER
3 tablespoons (30 g) rice flour
2 tablespoons (30–35 ml) water
A pinch of baking soda

1 Mix the Batter ingredients together in a bowl.
2 Slice the green beans into small pieces. Mix with the natto until they are coated.
3 Add the natto mixture to the Batter. Heat some oil to 340–360°F (170–180°C) and drop spoonfuls of the mixture into the oil. Deep fry until golden brown. Drain off the oil and serve with grated ginger and soy sauce.

Mountain Yam White Miso Soup

Serves 2

½ mountain yam (3½ oz/100 g)
2 to 3 tablespoons (35 to 50 g) white miso (see page
    15 for a homemade recipe)
One 2-inch (5-cm) piece dried kombu seaweed
1⅔ cups (400 ml) water
A pinch of sea salt

Substitutions: Use any other type of root vegetable
like baby potatoes, daikon or turnip if mountain yam is
not available. Use 1½ tablespoons of another type of
miso instead of the white miso.

1   Make the kombu seaweed water by immersing the
dried kombu seaweed in 1⅔ cups (400 ml) water, and
refrigerating it overnight. (Put the leftover kombu
seaweed in your rice bran pickling bed.)
2   Peel and cut the mountain yam into ¼-inch (5-mm)
slices and soak in a bowl of water. Drain and put into a
pan, add the kombu seaweed water and a pinch of salt,
and heat over medium heat. When it comes to a boil
skim the surface and cook until the mountain yam is
translucent. Dissolve the miso in some of the cooking
liquid in a separate small bowl or in the ladle, then add
to the soup.

NOTE Mountain yam is
available at Asian grocery
stores or use whatever
root vegetables are
available locally like baby
potatoes, daikon or turnip.

Mixed "Black" Rice

Serves 2

1 cup (150 g) uncooked white rice
1 tablespoon black or red rice
1 cup (240 ml) water
A pinch of sea salt

1   Rinse the rice and black
rice, and put into a pan with
1 cup (240 ml) water. Let it
soak for 1 hour.
2   Heat the pan over high
with the lid on until it comes
to a boil and add a pinch of

salt. Turn the heat down very low, cover and cook for
15 minutes. Turn off the heat and leave it to steam and
rest for another 15 minutes.

Clams Simmered in Amazake

Mitsuba Rice

Clam Stock with Tofu

Simmering shellfish in amazake makes it plump and juicy. Aromatic and luxurious, this is a great one-dish meal. If you don't have mitsuba leaves, use seasonal leafy greens for the rice instead.

Clam Stock with Tofu

Serves 2 to 3

All the reserved steaming liquid
    from the clams (see recipe on
    facing page)
1²⁄₃ to 2½ cups (400 to 600 ml)
    water
Light soy sauce, to taste
1 block (10 oz/300 g) silken tofu
Finely minced green onion,
    to garnish

1 Cut the tofu into small cubes. Put the clam steaming liquid in a pan, add the water and bring to a boil over medium heat. Skim the surface if there is any residue.
2 Add the tofu and heat through. Adjust the seasoning with the light soy sauce. Ladle into bowls and scatter green onions on top.

NOTE Use a wide-bottomed ladle or sieve with handle to lightly skim the surface.

Clams Simmered in Amazake

Shelf life: 4 TO 5 DAYS IN THE REFRIGERATOR

2¼ lbs (1 kg) fresh Manila or littleneck clams in their shells
   (or ⅓ lb/150 g clam meats without the shells)
4 cups (1 liter) water
2 tablespoons sea salt
6 tablespoons sake
½ red chili pepper, sliced into rounds

A INGREDIENTS
1½ tablespoons soy sauce
3 tablespoons (50 g) amazake, concentrated type (see
   page 11 for a homemade recipe)
1½ tablespoons (15 g) finely minced ginger

1   Put the clams into a pot with the water and salt and leave for 1 hour to eliminate the sand. Throw out the salt water, put the clams in fresh water, and leave them to soak for about 10 minutes. Drain in a colander.
2   Put the clams and sake in a pan, cover and heat over medium. Shake the pan occasionally for 2 to 3 minutes until the clams open up.

3   Drain into a colander (reserving the steaming liquid) and allow to cool, then remove the clam meats from the shells.
4   Put the A ingredients and 2 tablespoons of the steaming liquid into a pan and mix quickly. Heat over medium to reduce the liquid. When it has thickened, add the clam meats and chili pepper and cook quickly for a couple more minutes.

Mitsuba Rice

Serves 2

¾ cup + 1 tablespoon (200 ml)
   water
1 cup (150 g) uncooked white rice
1 tablespoon sake
1 teaspoon light soy sauce
1 cup (30 g) mitsuba or other dark
   leafy greens in season (like
   Italian parsley, coriander leaves
   or baby spinach)
2 pinches of sea salt

1   Rinse the rice and place it in a pot with the water. Let it soak for an hour.
2   Add the sake and soy sauce. Heat the pan over high with the lid on until it comes to a boil and add a pinch of salt. Turn the heat down very low, cover and cook for 15 minutes. Turn off the heat and leave it to steam and rest for 15 more minutes.
3   Finely chop the mitsuba or other greens and sprinkle with the salt. Squeeze out the excess moisture and mix into the hot rice.

NOTE Mitsuba is available at Asian grocery stores.

Mackerel and Amazake Curry with Iced Lemon Lassi

Mackerel and Amazake Curry

Amazake Lemon Lassi Drink

You can easily make a thick, sweet and tasty curry without using wheat flour. How about this meal on a hot day or for a busy weekday dinner?

Mackerel and Amazake Curry

Serves 2

6 oz (180 g) canned mackerel in
    water
¼ medium onion
1 garlic clove
One ½-inch (1¼-cm) piece ginger
½ medium tomato or 1 plum
    tomato
1 teaspoon cumin seeds
1 tablespoon vegetable oil
2 servings cooked warm rice
    (about 2 cups/400 g)

A INGREDIENTS
1 to 1½ tablespoons curry powder
2 to 3 tablespoons (35 to 50 g)
    amazake, concentrated type (see
    page 11 for a homemade recipe)
2 teaspoons soy sauce

GARNISHES
Fresh coriander leaves, lemon
    slices, tomato, red onion,
    avocado cubes

1 Finely mince the onion, garlic and ginger. Dice the tomato.
2 Heat the oil, garlic, ginger and cumin seeds in a pan over low.
3 When it's fragrant, add the onion, raise the heat to medium and sauté until golden brown. Add the tomato and sauté some more.
4 Add the canned mackerel with the can juices to the **A** ingredients and simmer until the liquid has been reduced. Serve over rice with the garnishes.

NOTE The addition of tomatoes gives the dish a subtle sourness as well as a refreshing taste.

Amazake Lemon Lassi Drink

Serves 2

¾ cup (150 g) amazake, concentrated type
    (see page 11 for a homemade recipe)
⅔ cup (150 ml) soy milk
2 tablespoons lemon juice
Grated lemon zest, to taste
Ice

Blend all the ingredients, except the ice, until creamy. Pour into glasses filled with ice. If you don't have ice, thin out the mixture with ice cold water to the desired consistency.

Seafood and Soy Milk Yogurt Curry with Lemon Rice and Yogurt Marinated Cabbage

Red Cabbage Marinated in Yogurt ➡ Page 43

Lemon Rice ➡ Page 43

Seafood and Soy Milk Yogurt Curry ➡ Page 42

My seafood of choice here is bluefish or mackerel. I recommend marinating it in yogurt, cooking it with spices and serving it as a refreshing, energy-giving curry.

Homemade Soy Milk Yogurt

Soy milk yogurt is a non-dairy version that can be used in a wide variety of ways, just like regular yogurt. It adds a richness to dishes, including desserts. Of course, commercially available products are also fine, but it's easy to make your own.

Shelf life: 4 TO 5 DAYS IN THE REFRIGERATOR

4 cups (1 liter) unsweetened soy milk
1 packet yogurt starter or culture (1 g)

NOTE You can buy yogurt starter at a local market or health food store, or order it online.

Instructions

1 Add the yogurt starter to the soy milk carton.

2 Close up the cap, and shake well to mix.

3 Wrap in a yogurt warmer. (If using a yogurt maker, turn it on for 6 to 8 hours at 113°F/45°C).

4 It's done when it coagulates. The longer you keep it, the more sour it becomes.

Uses for Homemade Soy Milk Yogurt

➡ LIGHT POTATO SALAD
Mix boiled potatoes with oil, salt, grated garlic and soy yogurt for a lighter result than potato salad made with mayonnaise.

➡ MAKING YOGURT-LIKE CHEESE If you weigh down the freshly made yogurt and drain it while it's still warm, you can make a thick, creamy yogurt that is denser than commercially available yogurt. It can be used like ricotta cheese for salads, breads and sandwiches.

Seafood and Soy Milk Yogurt Curry

In addition to sardines—mackerel, bluefish, swordfish, shrimp, squid or scallops are delicious in this dish, so use any kind of seafood you like.

Serves 2

½ lb (225 g) fresh sardines, cleaned, scaled and gutted
1 medium onion
1 medium tomato
2 garlic cloves
½-inch (1¼-cm) piece ginger
1 red chili pepper, deseeded
⅔ cup (150 g) Homemade Soy Milk Yogurt (page 41) plus more for marinade
2 tablespoons mirin
1 tablespoon curry powder
1 teaspoon sea salt
3 tablespoons vegetable oil

GARNISHES
Lemon slices, roughly chopped lettuce, minced parsley

Cut the heads off the sardines, wash well and pat dry. Spread soy milk yogurt on both sides and refrigerate for at least 15 minutes, up to overnight. Finely mince the garlic cloves, ginger, onion and tomato.

Sauté the oil, garlic, ginger and chili pepper in a pan over low heat. When fragrant, add the onions, increase the heat and sauté until golden brown. Add the tomatoes, curry powder and salt and mix quickly.

Add the marinated sardines from Step 1, the ⅔ cup (150 g) of soy milk yogurt and the mirin. Bring to a boil, then turn the heat down to low and simmer for about 10 minutes. Adjust the seasoning with salt or soy sauce. Serve with the Lemon Rice (see page 43) and lemon slices and chopped lettuce, and sprinkle with the parsley.

NOTE Sardines tend to fall apart, so cook them gently while spooning the sauce over them.

Red Cabbage Marinated in Yogurt

Serves 2

1½ cups (150 g) red cabbage
½ cup (30 g) red onion
½ teaspoon sea salt
¼ cup (50 g) Homemade Soy Milk Yogurt (see page 41)
2 teaspoons (10 g) amazake, concentrated type (see page 11 for a homemade recipe)

1 Shred the cabbage. Slice the onion thinly. Sprinkle salt over both and let stand at least a half hour.
2 Squeeze out the excess moisture and mix with the soy milk yogurt and amazake.

Lemon Rice

Serves 2

2¼ cups (450 g) firm cooked rice
1 tablespoon vegetable oil
1 to 1½ tablespoons lemon juice (or the juice of ½ lemon)
Salt and pepper, to taste

A INGREDIENTS
1 garlic clove, minced
1 teaspoon cumin seeds
½ teaspoon turmeric

1 Put the oil and the **A** ingredients in a frying pan, and heat over low until the oil starts to bubble.
2 Add the rice and stir-fry quickly. Add the lemon juice and stir-fry until there is no moisture left in the pan. Season to taste with salt and pepper.

Kimchi and Tofu Rice Bowl with Vegetable Miso Soup

Kimchi and Tofu Rice Bowl

Homemade Cabbage Amazake Kimchi

Spring Vegetable Miso Soup

Use umami-packed kimchi as the centerpiece of a spicy fermented meal. The kimchi can be made with daikon radish or turnip instead of cabbage.

Homemade Cabbage Amazake Kimchi

Kimchi is the perfect accompaniment to rice. The one on the left in the photo is a mild version made with Korean red pepper. The one on the right is spicy, made with chili pepper powder.

Shelf life: **1 WEEK IN THE REFRIGERATOR**

½ head cabbage (about 1 lb 2 oz/500 g), cored
2 teaspoons sea salt
4 cloves garlic, crushed or finely minced
¼ medium apple (2 oz/50 g)
1½ tablespoons grated ginger

A INGREDIENTS
¼ cup (50 g) amazake, concentrated type (see page 11 for a recipe)
3 to 4 tablespoons mild ground Korean red pepper (or 1 to 1½ teaspoons red pepper powder)
1 tablespoon fish sauce
¼ to ⅓ teaspoon sea salt

NOTES
• If you don't have fish sauce, you can use soy sauce plus a small packet of katsuobushi (bonito flakes).
• If you want to make it a little sweeter, add more amazake.

1 Core the cabbage and slice it into large pieces. Put into a plastic bag. Add the 2 teaspoons of salt, shake well, and leave for at least 15 minutes until the cabbage is wilted.
2 Crush the garlic and grate the apple and ginger into a bowl. Add the **A** ingredients and mix well.
3 Squeeze the cabbage repeatedly in the bag. Take it out of the bag, squeeze out and drain off the water, and put it back in the bag. Add the Step 2 mixture and mix well.
4 Press the air from the plastic bag, tie it up and let it rest overnight in the refrigerator.

Spring Vegetable Miso Soup

Serves 2

4 asparagus stalks
¼ medium onion
1⅔ cups (400 ml) water
1 teaspoon fish sauce
2 tablespoons (35 g) white or light brown miso (see page 15 for a homemade recipe) or 1 heaping teaspoon (10 g) regular miso

NOTE Fish sauce is a Japanese staple. A half teaspoon in water makes an excellent stock for miso soup. Thai or Vietnamese fish sauce also works well.

1 Cut the asparagus into 2-inch (5-cm) pieces. Slice the onion thinly.
2 Heat the water, fish sauce and onion in a small pan over low heat. When the onion is translucent, add the asparagus and heat through. Dissolve the miso in some of the cooking liquid in a separate small bowl or in the ladle, then add it to the soup.

Kimchi and Tofu Rice Bowl

Mixed "Black" Rice (see page 35)
Homemade Cabbage Amazake Kimchi (above)
Silken tofu
Shirasu (cooked salted whitebait, optional)
Green onion, minced
Sesame oil
Soy sauce
(all amounts are to taste)

Put the warm Mixed "Black Rice" in a bowl. Top with kimchi, tofu, fish and green onion. Drizzle with soy sauce and sesame oil. (This tastes best when the rice is hot and the toppings are cold.)

Mirin Pickles with Amazake Fruit Yogurt

Amazake Fruit Yogurt

Pickled Bean Tapanade

Homemade Mirin Pickles (bell peppers and onion; beans, burdock root and mushrooms)

If you have pickles on hand, you can quickly make a healthy breakfast or lunch. The key is to create a variety of textures to choose from and combine.

Amazake Fruit Yogurt

Serves 2

¾ cup (200 g) Homemade Soy Milk Yogurt (see page 41 for a homemade recipe)

½ cup (100 g) amazake, concentrated type (see page 11 for a homemade recipe)

1 kiwi fruit, peeled and chopped, or any other fruit like banana or mango

Add the amazake to the soy milk yogurt and mix until smooth. Top with chopped kiwi (or other fruit of your choice) and mix in while eating.

Homemade Mirin Pickles

Pickles with a crunchy texture and delicious taste are flavored with mirin (sweet cooking sake) to give them a sweet-sour tang. These make a wonderful snack served with lettuce, bread and Amazake Fruit Yogurt. They go very well with rice. Mirin burns easily, so be careful not to overcook it.

Shelf life: 1 MONTH IN THE REFRIGERATOR

Pickled Beans, Burdock Root and Mushrooms

2 cups (200 g) boiled beans of your choice (soybeans, chickpeas, kidney beans, etc.)
1 cup (150 g) sliced burdock root
1 cup (75 g) shimeji mushrooms

PICKLING LIQUID
⅔ cup (150 ml) mirin (sweet cooking wine)
⅔ cup (150 ml) rice vinegar
3 tablespoons soy sauce
1 garlic clove
1 bay leaf

1 Scrape the skin off the burdock root and cut it into 2-inch (5-cm) lengths. Slice each piece into 2 to 4 narrow pieces lengthwise, and place them in a bowl of water. Break the shimeji mushrooms into small clumps. Slice the garlic clove.
2 Heat the Pickling Liquid ingredients in a small pan over low heat. When it bubbles lightly, add the burdock root and shimeji mushrooms and simmer gently for about 5 minutes while skimming the surface. Take the pan off the heat.
3 Put the beans in a preserving jar and pour in the Pickling Liquid and other ingredients while still hot. Cover and allow to cool. Store in the refrigerator.

Pickled Bell Pepper and Onion

2 large red or yellow bell peppers
¼ onion

PICKLING LIQUID
⅔ cup (150 ml) mirin
⅔ cup (150 ml) rice vinegar
3 tablespoons soy sauce
1 garlic clove
A few whole black peppercorns

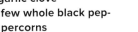

1 Slice the garlic clove. Heat in a small pan with the Pickling Liquid ingredients over low heat. Simmer gently for about 5 minutes. Take the pan off the heat and let cool.
2 Slice the onion thinly. Deseed the bell peppers and slice them into bite-size pieces. Put the onion and bell pepper into a preserving jar and pour in the Pickling Liquid.
3 Cover the jar. When the vegetables are wilted, press down on them firmly so that they're completely immersed in the Pickling Liquid. They're ready to eat the next day.

Pickled Bean Tapanade

Serves 2

1 cup (100 g) Pickled Beans, Burdock Root and Mushrooms (see above)
1 to 2 tablespoons olive oil, plus more for drizzling
1 tablespoon pickling liquid from the pickle jar
Salt, to taste

1 Place the pickles in a food processor or blender. (Adding some of the pickled garlic is also delicious.)
2 Add the olive oil and process until smooth. Season with a little of the pickling liquid and salt. Put into a serving bowl, drizzle with plenty of olive oil and spread on bread or wrap in lettuce leaves.

NOTE If you use a lot of beans, it becomes a hummus-like paste. And you can add more burdock root for texture!

Plum Miso Octopus with Ginger Rice, Kudzu Tofu and Zucchini Miso Soup

White Sesame Kudzu Tofu ➡ Page 50

Octopus and Cucumber with Plum Miso ➡ Page 51

Ginger Rice ➡ Page 51

Zucchini and Aburaage Miso Soup ➡ Page 51

A refreshing menu featuring handmade kudzu tofu and ume plum miso. The kudzu tofu is even more delicious if you change up the flavors with the toppings as you eat it.

Refreshing Plum or Apricot Miso

This miso has an appetizing sweet-and-sour flavor imparted by the fruit. Its richness makes it easy to pair with most foods, and as an added bonus, it keeps for a long time.

Shelf life: 3 MONTHS IN THE REFRIGERATOR OR A YEAR IN THE FREEZER

⅔ lb (300 g) ripe Japanese ume plums or unripe apricots

1¼ cups (300 g) brown miso (see page 13 for a home-made recipe)

½ cup (100 g) amazake, concentrated type (see page 11 for a homemade recipe)

Instructions

1
Wash the ume plums and pat them dry. Remove the stem bases with a skewer or paring knife.

2
Put the ume plums in a freezer bag, and keep in the freezer overnight. (This makes them fall apart easier.)

3
Put the miso and amazake in a bowl and mix well.

4
Put one-third of the miso mixture in the bottom of a glass preserving container with cover. Add the frozen plums and cover with the rest of the miso mixture. (If you have a deep container, fill it with alternating layers of the miso mixture and the plums, finishing with a layer of the miso mixture.)

5
Cover the container, and leave out overnight until the plums defrost and water rises up to the surface.

6
Mix well with a large spoon. Mix once a day; it is ready to eat after 3 days. Store in the refrigerator, and mix it up every time you use it.

NOTES I've suggested unripe apricots as an alternative to the Japanese ume plums since they may not be readily available where you live.
If you're not going to use the miso for a while, take the pits out of the fruit. You won't need to stir it daily, and the miso will keep longer.

➡ **LEEKS WITH PLUM MISO SAUCE** Cut leeks into 2-inch (5-cm) lengths and blanch them quickly in boiling water, about a minute. Mix with some of the Refreshing Plum or Apricot Miso. The miso can also be served on fresh squid or tuna. It can be used like a traditional Japanese condiment called vinegar miso on konnyaku jelly, sashimi-quality squid and more.

White Sesame Kudzu Tofu

Serves 2–3

2½ tablespoons (20 g) kudzu or kuzu
flour
4 teaspoons (20 g) sesame paste or
tahini
1 tablespoon sake
A pinch of sea salt
1 cup plus 2 teaspoons (250 ml) water

TOPPINGS
Grated wasabi or wasabi paste, soy
sauce, **Refreshing Plum or Apricot
Miso** (see page 49)

1 Put the flour, sesame paste, sake and salt in a pan and mix well with a spatula. Add the water a little at a time to thin out the mixture.
2 Heat the contents on medium heat while stirring constantly. When it comes to a boil, turn the heat to low and cook gently while stirring constantly for 3 to 4 minutes. When the batter thickens and stretches, take the pan off the heat.
3 Pour the batter into two small molds. Cool to room temperature, then refrigerate until firm. Eat with grated wasabi, soy sauce and/or Refreshing Plum or Apricot Miso on top.

NOTE Kudzu or kudzu flour is made from the root of the kudzu vine, and is available online (also known as kudzu powder). Arrowroot or tapioca flour can be used as a substitute.

Octopus and Cucumber with Plum Miso

Serves 2

⅓ lb (150 g) boiled octopus
1 Japanese cucumber or 2 pick-
    ling gherkins
2 pinches of sea salt
¼ medium onion
⅛ cup (30 g) wakame seaweed,
    soaked and reconstituted
Refreshing Plum or Apricot
    Miso (see page 49), to serve

1 Cut the cucumber in half, sprinkle with salt and roll it firmly several times on a cutting board. Let stand for 15 minutes, then squeeze out the excess moisture. Cut into bite-sized pieces. Slice the onion, put into a bowl of water for a few minutes, then drain.
2 Cut the boiled octopus and wakame seaweed into bite-sized pieces. Put everything on a plate, and spoon over some Refreshing Plum or Apricot Miso or serve on the side.

Zucchini and Aburaage Miso Soup

Serves 2

½ medium zucchini
1 piece aburaage fried tofu
    (¾ oz/20 g)
1⅔ cups (400 ml) kombu seaweed
    water (see page 35)
1½ to 2 tablespoons (30 to 35 g)
    brown miso (see page 13 for a
    homemade recipe)

1 Cut the aburaage sheet in half lengthwise then slice finely. Cut the zucchini in half lengthwise then slice thinly into small moons.
2 Put the kombu seaweed water in a small pan and bring to a boil. Add the aburaage and zucchini and cook briefly. Dissolve the miso in some of the cooking liquid in a separate small bowl or in the ladle, then add to the soup.

Ginger Rice

1½ cups (300 g) uncooked white
    rice
1½ tablespoons sake
½ teaspoon sea salt
½ teaspoon soy sauce
1 tablespoon (30 g) ginger or 2 tea-
    spoons (20 g) regular ginger
Finely shredded kombu seaweed,
    to taste

1 Wash the rice and put it into a pot with water to cover. Let it soak for an hour. Finely shred the ginger.
2 Drain the rice. Put it back in the pot with 1⅔ cups (400 ml) Add the sake, salt and soy sauce and mix. Top with the ginger and kombu seaweed. Heat the pan over high with the lid on until it comes to a boil. Turn the heat down very low, cover and cook for 15 min-utes. Turn off the heat and leave to steam and rest for 10 minutes. Mix well before serving.

Soba with Green Chili Miso and Eggplant Sautéed in Ume Vinegar

Eggplant Sautéed in Ume Vinegar ➡ Page 55

Green Chili Miso, Spinach and Natto Soba Noodles ➡ Page 54

The miso mated with the flavor of green chili peppers, then paired with the nalta jute, is delicious and invigorating. The refreshingly spicy and sour fermented ingredients are the perfect accompaniment!

Fragrant Green Chili Miso

A miso with a refreshing yet lingering spiciness, this version can be eaten as a summer side dish. It is made with amazake and aromatic shiso leaves, and the green chili is gently fried to make it less spicy and more fragrant.

Shelf life: 1 MONTH IN THE REFRIGERATOR

½ cup (75 g) minced green chili peppers

10 green shiso leaves (available at Asian grocery stores)

5 tablespoons (80 g) Homemade Brown Rice Miso (see page 13 for a homemade recipe)

4 tablespoons (65 g) amazake, concentrated type (see page 11 for a homemade recipe)

2 tablespoons sesame oil

Instructions

1 Split the chili peppers in half lengthwise and remove the seeds (if you include the seeds, the miso will be extremely spicy). Finely mince along with the green shiso leaves.

2 Put the sesame oil and chili peppers in a frying pan and stir-fry over low heat. If you stir-fry the chili peppers slowly, the spiciness will be reduced.

3 Add the miso and amazake and heat through for 1 to 2 minutes until it's no longer watery.

4 Turn off the heat, add the green shiso leaves and mix well.

Uses for Fragrant Green Chili Miso

➡ **AS A RICE BALL FILLING** This green chili miso is great with rice as well as with soba or somen noodles. It's perfect as a filling for onigiri (rice balls). You can put it into bento lunch boxes too.

➡ **SPREAD ON PANFRIED EGGPLANT OR TOFU** Spread it on eggplant that has been panfried until golden brown to make a great side dish. If you use the miso as a topping on tofu, you can serve it as is as a snack.

Green Chili Miso, Spinach and Natto Soba Noodles

This soba noodle dish does not require a dipping sauce: just top the noodles with chopped spinach, green onion, sliced onion, bonito flakes, Fragrant Green Chili Miso and some soy sauce. It's delicious and also very healthy!

Serves 2

2 cups (50 g) jute leaves or baby spinach (also known as nalta jute or jute mallow; available at Middle Eastern or Asian grocery stores)
¼ medium red onion
Green onions, to taste
2 packets natto (3 oz/90 g)
½ lb (200 g) dried soba noodles
Fragrant Green Chili Miso (see page 53), to taste
Katsuobushi (skipjack tuna or bonito flakes), to garnish
Soy sauce, to drizzle

NOTE Chop up the jute leaves into small pieces. If you can't find it, use spinach instead.

1 Blanch the jute leaves briefly, about 2 to 3 minutes, then drain and immerse in cold water. Drain again and squeeze out the excess water. Chop the leaves with a knife blade or cleaver. Slice the onion thinly and finely mince the green onion. Finely chop the natto.

2 Boil the soba noodles, drain and rinse in cold water. Drain agan and arrange on serving plates. Top with the jute leaves, green onion, Fragrant Green Chili Miso, natto and katsuobushi flakes, and drizzle with soy sauce.

Eggplant Sautéed in Ume Vinegar

Ume vinegar is rice vinegar infused with the sweet-sour flavor of preserved ume plums. You can buy it in an Asian food store or make your own. When added to stir-fried eggplant with garlic, chili, soy sauce and amazake, it is absolutely delicious!

Serves 2

3 Asian eggplants (1 lb/450 g)
1 garlic clove
1 tablespoon vegetable oil
1 red chili pepper, deseeded
1 tablespoon (15 g) amazake, con-centrated type (see page 11 for a homemade recipe)
2 teaspoons ume vinegar (avail-able at Asian grocery stores or online)
Soy sauce, to taste
Black pepper, to taste

1 Make several slits in the skins of the eggplants and cut them into bite-sized pieces. Soak them in a 3 percent solution of saltwater (½ teaspoon salt per cup of water). Slice the garlic clove.

2 Drain the eggplant and squeeze out as much water as you can. Put the vegetable oil and garlic into a frying pan and sauté over low heat. Add the drained eggplant skin side down and sauté. Add the chili pepper too.

3 Add the amazake and continue to sauté. When it starts to brown, add the ume vinegar and mix with the eggplant. Season to taste with soy sauce and black pepper.

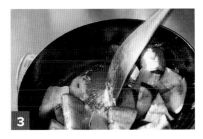

NOTE Amazake burns easily, so add it at the end and reduce the heat.

Mixed Vegetable Sushi Rice and Tofu Topped with Fermented Ginger

Sushi Rice with Fermented
Ginger and Mixed Vegetables

Fermented Myoga Ginger and Regular Ginger

Tofu Topped with Fermented Ginger

This sugar-free mixed sushi is so refreshing. If you make the fermented condiments yourself, the marinade can be used as the vinegar for the sushi rice, and the condiments can be chopped and mixed into the rice or used as toppings.

Sushi Rice with Fermented Ginger and Mixed Vegetables

Use any vegetables in season. If you lightly panfry the vegetables, they'll become sweeter and slightly soft. Adding fermented ginger and its pickling juice to hot rice makes a deliciously sweet-sour rice!

Serves 2

1½ cups (300 g) hot cooked white rice
½ portion of Fermented Myoga Ginger and Regular Ginger (below)
2 tablespoons ginger pickling juice
½ ear corn
½ small zucchini
1 cup (160 g) edamame soybeans
Small dried fish (chirimenjako, available at Asian grocery stores), to taste (optional)
Roasted sesame seeds, to taste
1 tablespoon olive oil

1　Finely shred the fermented ginger and fermented myoga ginger, leaving some to use as decoration. Remove the kernels from the corn cob. Cut the zucchini into small dice. Boil the edamame in salt water and take the beans out of the pods.
2　Heat the olive oil in a frying pan. Stir-fry the zucchini, remove and set aside, then add and stir-fry the corn. Season both with a little salt.
3　Pour the ginger pickling juice over the hot cooked rice. Add the ginger, myoga ginger and sesame seeds and mix well. Scatter the chirimenjako and vegetables over the rice, and decorate with strips of the reserved myoga ginger.

Tofu Topped with Fermented Ginger

Serves 2

1 block (10 oz/300 g) tofu
Fermented Myoga Ginger and

Regular Ginger, to taste (see below)
Soy sauce, to taste
Sesame oil, to taste

Finely mince the ginger and myoga ginger and put on top of the tofu. Drizzle with soy sauce and sesame oil.

Fermented Myoga Ginger and Regular Ginger

Serves 2
Shelf life: 3 WEEKS IN THE REFRIGERATOR

5–6 bulbs (100 g) myoga ginger (available at Asian grocery stores)
1-inch (2.5-cm) piece ginger
Scant ½ cup (100 ml) red ume vinegar (available at Asian grocery stores)
Scant ½ cup (100 ml) mirin

1　Cut the myoga ginger buds in half lengthwise. Slice the ginger, put into a preserving container, and pour boiling water over them (see Note below).
2　Drain the ginger immediately and pat dry.
3　Put the mirin in a small pan over medium heat. When it bubbles lightly, turn the heat to low and cook for 2 minutes. Take off the heat and add the ume vinegar.
4　Put the gingers in a preserving container and pour the liquid from Step 3 over them. Cover with cling wrap, then secure the lid. Refrigerate. (It's ready to eat from the next day onward.)

NOTE Quickly blanching the ginger fixes the colors and makes them more vibrant when pickled. The photo to the left shows them when they are pickled without blanching.

Sea Bream and Pickled Daikon Sushi with Clear Broccolini Soup

Sea Bream and Pickled
Daikon Sushi ➡ Page 60

Clear Soup with Broccolini ➡ Page 61

Don't add any sugar to the sushi rice; instead utilize the sweetness of the Crunchy Dried Daikon Pickled with Amazake. This is a coloful menu, perfect for a festive occasion.

Crunchy Dried Daikon Pickled with Amazake

This is an easy version of takuan, a traditional Japanese pickle made with dried daikon radish that can be made in a plastic bag. The crunchy texture and mild flavor make these pickles addictive, even when eaten alone!

Shelf life: 2 WEEKS IN THE REFRIGERATOR

⅓ cup (40 g) dried sliced or shredded daikon (see Note)
1 small red chili, deseeded
Finely shredded kombu seaweed,
  to taste

PICKLING LIQUID
½ cup (100 g) amazake, concentrated type (see page 11 for a
  homemade recipe)
2 teaspoons rice vinegar
2 teaspoons soy sauce
⅔ teaspoon sea salt

Instructions

1 Put the dried daikon radish in a bowl and rinse briefly. Soak in water for 10 to 15 minutes to rehydrate it.

2 Drain into a colander while the daikon radish is still a bit tough. (Don't squeeze it out. The weight at this point will be about 4 oz or 100 g.)

3 Put the Pickling Liquid ingredients into a plastic bag and add the red chili pepper and shredded kombu seaweed.

4 Add the daikon and shake the bag several times to mix. Squeeze the air from the plastic bag and close it up. Refrigerate overnight. It is ready to eat the next day.

NOTE You can make your own dried daikon radish by peeling and slicing fresh daikon and placing it in a food dehydrator or in the oven at very low heat. You can also find a product called kiriboshi daikon, which is shredded dried daikon, at Asian grocery stores.

Sea Bream and Pickled Daikon Sushi

This treat can be made with sushi-grade salmon or boiled shrimp. Use several different types of fish to make a festive sushi platter!

Serves 2

⅓ lb (150 g) sea bream or other sashimi-grade fish
1 cup (150 g) uncooked white rice
2 tablespoons (30 g) Crunchy Dried Daikon Pickled
  with Amazake (see page 59), finely chopped
3 tablespoons mirin
2 tablespoons lemon juice or vinegar
½ teaspoon + ⅓ teaspoon sea salt
Toasted sesame seeds, to taste
1 radish, to garnish
Lemon zest, grated, to garnish

1 Put the mirin in a small pan and heat over very low heat. When it comes to a boil, cook for about 1 minute. Turn off the heat, add the lemon juice and ½ teaspoon salt and mix to dissolve to make the sushi vinegar.
2 Rinse the rice, and put it in a pan with ¾ cup (200 ml) water. Leave to soak for 1 hour. Heat the pan over high with the lid on, until it comes to a boil, then add a pinch of salt. Turn the heat down very low, then cover and cook for 15 minutes. Turn off the heat and let steam and rest for 15 minutes. Mix with the sushi vinegar, while it's still hot, then let cool.
3 Slice the sashimi thinly, sprinkle with ⅓ teaspoon salt and leave for 15 minutes. Pat the fish dry, line a shallow square container with kitchen parchment paper and place the sashimi slices on the paper.
4 Press ½ of the sushi rice into the container over the fish and scatter with the finely chopped Crunchy Dried Daikon Pickled with Amazake and toasted sesame seeds. Put in the rest of the sushi rice and press down.
5 Cover with cling wrap, place another square container of the same size into the first container and press down hard. Leave for the flavors to blend for a few minutes, turn the sushi onto a plate or cutting board, remove the parchment paper and slice into pieces. Top to taste with radish slices and scatter with grated zest.

NOTE As with the type of seafood you choose, you can also make this sushi using a variety of other pickled vegetables such as radish or turnip.

Clear Soup with Broccolini

Serves 2

¼ lb (115 g) broccolini florets
1⅔ cups (400 ml) kombu seaweed
   water (see page 35)
2 small packets katsuobushi (skipjack tuna or bonito flakes,
   1¾ oz/50 g)
1 tablespoon sake
1 tablespoon light soy sauce
Salt, to taste
Minced green onion, to taste
Dried wheat gluten (fu, available at
   Asian grocery stores), to taste

1 Blanch the broccolini florets, about 2 minutes, then drain and place in two soup bowls.
2 Bring the kombu seaweed water to a boil in a pan. Turn off the heat, add the katsuobushi flakes and wait for them to sink to the bottom of the pan. Strain the liquid through a sieve.
3 Return the strained liquid to the pan and add the sake and soy sauce. Bring to a boil, taste and adjust the seasoningwith salt, then ladle the soup into the bowls. Add green onion and fu, to taste.

PART 2

Fall and Winter Meals

As the weather gets colder, it becomes even easier to feel the power of fermentation. Soups and stews will warm you to the core as well as boost your immune system! Here are twelve fermented meals perfect for the time of year when root vegetables and mushrooms become especially delicious.

Tofu and Shiitake Bibimbap with Korean Style Vegetables and Leek Soup

Four Types of Namul ➡ Page 67

Tofu and Shiitake Mushroom Bibimbap ➡ Page 66

White Leek Soup ➡ Page 66

Here fermentation flair is added to the freshness and flavor of Korean cuisine. Your favorite vegetables can easily be transformed into namul (a versatile Korean vegetable side dish), which goes great with rice.

Homemade Amazake Gochujang

This is a quick homemade version of gochujang, the Korean spicy fermented bean paste, made with just three ingredients. You can put it on vegetables, add it to stir-fries for a spicy finish or use it in hot pots and soups. It's also delicious with some garlic or ginger added.

Shelf life: 2 MONTHS IN THE REFRIGERATOR

1 cup (100 g) amazake, concentrated type (see page 11 for a homemade recipe)
⅓ teaspoon (10 g) sea salt
1½ to 3 tablespoons (5–10 g) coarsely ground chili powder

NOTE If it's not well-mixed, it won't keep well, so make sure to stir it thoroughly.

Instructions

1 Put the salt and the chili powder in a bowl and mix well while crushing the salt.

2 Add the amazake and mix until smooth.

3 Cover the bowl and let it rest at room temperature overnight. It's done when it's firm. (The bowl on the left shows how it looks right after it's mixed; on the right, after standing overnight.)

Uses for Homemade Amazake Gochujang

➥ **AS A BASE FOR SAUCES**
It has a strong salty and pungent taste on its own, but when mixed with other seasonings, it tastes just right. It's tangy and delicious mixed with mayonnaise!

➥ **WITH NOODLES**
Add it to stir-fried noodles, somen or ramen. When finishing pasta, add a little to the boiling water to help emulsify the sauce.

➥ **FOR TOMATO-BASED SOUPS**
When added to tomato-based soups such as minestrone, the flavor becomes rich and spicy, giving it depth. It also works well with seafood and mushrooms.

Tofu and Shiitake Mushroom Bibimbap

Serves 2

1 block firm tofu (10 oz/300 g)
2 to 3 fresh shiitake mushrooms
1 garlic clove
1½ tablespoons sesame oil
1 tablespoon (18 g) amazake, concentrated type (see page 11 for a homemade recipe)
2 cups (400 g) cooked rice
Dollop of Homemade Amazake Gochujang (see page 65), to taste

1 Mince the shiitake mushrooms and garlic. Wrap the tofu in a kitchen towel and put a plate on top of it in the sink to press out the water.
2 Heat the sesame oil and garlic in a frying pan. When fragrant, add the shiitake mushrooms and sauté well. Add the tofu and sauté well until it's crumbly. Serve over the rice and top with Homemade Amazake Gochujang and Namul (see facing page).

NOTE Stir-fry the tofu thoroughly to give it a good texture, if not a crispy, seared crust.

White Leek Soup

Serves 2

The white part of 1 medium leek
Scant ½ cup (100 ml) soy milk
Salt and pepper, to taste

A INGREDIENTS
1¼ cups (300 ml) kombu seaweed water (page 35)
2 teaspoons (10 g) amazake, concentrated type (see page 11 for a homemade recipe)
½ teaspoon sea salt

1 Cut the leek into thin diagonal slices.
2 Put the **A** ingredients and the leek into a pan over medium heat and bring to a boil. Cook for about 2 minutes and skim the surface. Add the soy milk and heat through. Season to taste with salt and pepper.

Four Types of Namul

Namul is a Korean vegetable side dish made with shredded or blanched and lightly seasoned fresh vegetables. These are colorful and very healthy as well as delicious!

Daikon Namul

Serves 2

1⅔ cups (200 g) shredded daikon
1 teaspoon sea salt

A INGREDIENTS
1 tablespoon ground sesame seeds
2 teaspoons sesame oil
1 teaspoon rice vinegar

Salt, to taste

Peel and finely shred the daikon radish with a mandolin and put it in a bowl. Sprinkle with the salt and leave it for at least 15 minutes. Squeeze out the excess moisture. Add the **A** ingredients and combine. Adjust the seasoning with salt.

Carrot Namul

Serves 2

½ medium carrot
2 pinches of sea salt

A INGREDIENTS
2 teaspoons ground sesame seeds
1 teaspoon sesame oil
1 teaspoon rice vinegar
1 teaspoon (5 g) amazake, concentrated type (see page 11 for a homemade recipe)

Salt, to taste

Finely shred the carrot using a mandolin and place it in a bowl. Sprinkle with salt and leave for at least 15 minutes. Squeeze out the excess moisture. Add the **A** ingredients and combine. Adjust the seasoning with salt.

Bean Sprout Namul

Serves 2

1 cup (120 g) bean sprouts
½ teaspoon sea salt

A INGREDIENTS
2 teaspoons ground sesame seeds
1 teaspoon sesame oil
1 teaspoon rice vinegar
½ teaspoon soy sauce
Grated garlic, to taste

Salt, to taste

Put about 1 cup of water in a small pan and bring to a boil. Add the bean sprouts and the salt, cover and cook over medium heat for 5 to 6 minutes. Drain the water, return the bean sprouts to the pan and cook until the moisture is gone. Add the **A** ingredients and mix. Season to taste with salt.

Spinach Namul

Serves 2

3 cups (100 g) spinach leaves
½ teaspoon sea salt

A INGREDIENTS
1 tablespoon ground sesame seeds
2 teaspoons sesame oil
½ teaspoon soy sauce
Grated garlic, to taste

Additional soy sauce, to taste

Blanch the spinach for about a minute, then drain and place in cold water. Drain again, squeeze tightly to remove the water and slice into 1-inch (2.5-cm) pieces. Put it in a bowl, sprinkle with the salt and let it stand for at least 10 minutes. Squeeze out any excess moisture. Add the **A** ingredient and combine, adjusting the seasoning with soy sauce.

Root Vegetable Miso Soup with Millet Rice and Miso Pickles

Glutinous Millet Rice

Root Vegetable Soup with Brown Rice Miso

Diced Vegetables Pickled in Miso

This meal celebrates and elevates root vegetables. Handmade miso not only tastes good, it settles the stomach. You can easily pickle your vegetables in miso without making a rice bran bed.

Root Vegetable Soup with Brown Rice Miso

Serves 4

1 cup (150 g) daikon, diced
½ medium carrot
1 cup (150 g) taro root or yam,
   diced
1 teaspoon sea salt
1 cup (150 g) lotus root, diced
½ medium onion
2 pieces aburaage (thin fried tofu)
1 tablespoon sesame oil
4 cups (1 liter) kombu seaweed
   water (see page 35)
½ teaspoon sea salt
3 tablespoons (50 g) Homemade
   Brown Rice Miso (see page 13
   for a homemade recipe)
1 cup (30 g) blanched spinach
Minced green onions, to garnish

1 Peel and dice the vegetables. Sprinkle the taro with ½ teaspoon salt.
2 Add the sesame oil and vegetables to a pan and sauté well. Turn off the heat, add the salt and let stand for at least 10 minutes until the moisture is released from the vegetables.
3 Add the kombu seaweed water to the pan, turn on the heat and bring to a boil. Skim the surface and simmer over low heat until the vegetables are tender or partially cooked, however you prefer them.
4 Add the aburaage. Dissolve the miso in some of the cooking liquid in a separate small bowl or in the ladle, then add to the soup. Top with the blanched greens and green onion.

Diced Vegetables Pickled in Miso

Serves 2

1 cup (150 g) diced daikon and
   carrot
2 teaspoons (10 g) Homemade
   Brown Rice Miso (see page 13
   for a homemade recipe)
⅓ teaspoon sea salt
½ teaspoon rice vinegar

1 Cut the daikon into ½-inch (1.5-cm) dice and the carrot into slightly smaller dice.
2 Put all the ingredients into a plastic bag and mix well. Let stand for about 15 minutes, then drain off the excess water.
3 Expel the air. Close up the bag and allow to pickle in the refrigerator overnight.

Glutinous Millet Rice

Serves 2

1 cup (150 g) uncooked partially
   milled rice
1 tablespoon glutinous millet
A pinch of sea salt

1 Rinse the rice and millet, drain and place in a pot with ¾ cup water. Add the salt and let it soak for at least 30 minutes.
2 Heat the pan over high until the water comes to a boil. Turn the heat down as low as possible, and simmer for 15 minutes. Take the pan off the heat and leave the rice to steam and rest for 15 minutes.

Panfried Fish and Vegetables Marinated in Sake Lees with Bean Sprout Soup and Sake Lees Pickles

Panfried Fish Marinated in Sake Lees ➡ Page 72

Vegetables Pickled in Sake Lees ➡ Page 73

Bean Sprout and Sake Lees Soup ➡ Page 73

Sake lees bring out the flavor and richness of food. Here this fabulous fermented ingredient is featured as an easy-to-use pickling or marinating bed for a fish dish, a vegetable side and even a soup.

Sake Lees Pickling Base (Kasudoko)

This is a sake lees pickling or marinating base with the sweetness of mirin and the umami of miso and kombu seaweed. I recommend using it for any kind of fish, squid or shrimp. Delicious!

Shelf life: 1 MONTH IN THE REFRIGERATOR

1 cup (200 g) sake lees (available at Asian grocery stores)
⅓ cup (100 g) white miso (see page 15 for a homemade recipe)
3 to 5 tablespoons mirin
1 teaspoon sea salt
1 to 2 red chilis or jalapeno peppers, sliced into rounds
Finely shredded kombu seaweed, to taste

Instructions

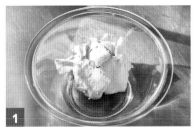

1 Put the sake lees and mirin in a bowl.

2 Mix well with a whisk or a spatula.

3 Add the white miso and the salt, and mix some more.

4 Add the red chili pepper and the kombu seaweed and mix quickly. Transfer to a preserving container.

Panfried Fish Marinated in Sake Lees

Once you try making your own sake lees marinades or pickles, you won't be able to stop because they're so delicious!

Serves 2

½ lb (250 g) seabass, cod, mahi-mahi, tuna or tilapia
1 cup (200 g) sliced kabocha squash or pumpkin
½ medium bell pepper
5 tablespoons (80 g) Sake Lees Pickling Base (see page 71)
A pinch of sea salt

1 Sprinkle the fish with salt and leave for about 30 minutes, then pat dry. Spread the Sake Lees Pickling Base on a piece of cling wrap, place the fish on top, spread more of the Sake Lees Pickling Base on top of the fish and wrap up. Marinate in the refrigerator for at least one night, up to 3 days.
2 Cut the vegetables into easy-to-eat pieces. Scrape the Sake Lees Pickling Base off the fish (reserving it for the soup on the next page). Panfry the fish and the vegetables over low heat in a frying pan until done.

> **NOTE** When marinating fish or meat in sake lees, instead of putting the pieces directly into the base, it's a good idea to spread some of the base on a piece of cling wrap and then wrap them up to avoid contaminating the base.

Vegetables Pickled in Sake Lees

¼ medium daikon
2 small Japanese cucumbers or pickling
  gherkins
1 medium carrot
1 portion Sake Lees Pickling Base (see
  page 71)
1 teaspoon sea salt

1   Slice the vegetables into strips. Sprinkle with salt and leave for at least a half hour, then drain well.
2   Put the vegetables and base in a pickling container and pickle the vegetables at least overnight or up to 1 week.

NOTES
• If you pickle the vegetables for a long time, they'll taste like a traditional Japanese pickle called narazuke.
• The vegetables are also delicious sliced without removing the sake lees.

Bean Sprout and Sake Lees Soup

Serves 2

1 garlic clove, minced
1 teaspoon minced or grated ginger
1¾ cups (200 g) bean sprouts
5 tablespoons (80 g) Sake Lees Pickling Base (Kasudoko) left over from marinating the fish (page 71)
1⅔ cups (400 ml) water
Salt, to taste

1   Put the garlic and ginger in a small pan over low heat. When it's fragrant, add the bean sprouts. Raise the heat to medium and stir-fry until the sprouts are translucent.
2   Add the Sake Lees Pickling Base and mix quickly. Add the water and bring to a boil. Simmer over low heat for 5 minutes while skimming the surface. Season to taste with salt.

Creamy Oysters Sautéed in Sake Lees and Soy Milk with Peppers Marinated in Ume Vinegar

Bell Peppers Marinated in Ume Vinegar ➡ Page 77

Creamy Oysters Sautéed in Sake Lees and Soy Milk ➡ Page 77

This is a warming stew that harnesses the richness of sake lees. It's delicious served over rice or with bread. As a side dish, I've paired it with peppers marinated in a refreshing ume-vinegar infusion.

Sake Lees Paste

This recipe turns body-warming sake lees into a versatile paste that's smooth and easy to dissolve. Since it has salt in it, it also keeps for a longer time than plain sake lees, which is a big plus.

Shelf life: 3 MONTHS IN THE REFRIGERATOR / 1 YEAR IN THE FREEZER

1 cup (200 g) sake lees (available at an Asian grocery store)
1 tablespoon sea salt
2 teaspoons vegetable oil

Instructions

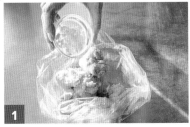

Put the sake lees and the salt in a plastic bag.

Knead the bag until the mixture is smooth. If the sake lees are hard, add about 1 teaspoon of sake.

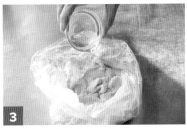

Add the oil and knead some more.

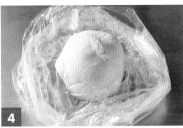

When the paste coheres, either store it in the plastic bag by eliminating all the air and closing it tightly or transfer it to a preserving container. Refrigerate in both cases.

Uses for Sake Lees Paste

➡ **AS A FLAVOR BOOSTER IN STEWS** If you get bored with your usual stews, add just a little bit of this paste for depth of flavor and richness.

➡ **IN A WARMING SOUP** Just add fish or root vegetables with some miso and sake lees paste to make kasujiru, a traditional soup. It warms you to your core, and is perfect as a winter starter!

➡ **TO REDUCE YOUR SALT INTAKE** Although this paste is low in salt, it's full of flavor so it's recommended for people who want to reduce their salt intake. It's delicious when added to stir-fries with meat, fish or vegetables.

Creamy Oysters Sautéed in Sake Lees and Soy Milk

The aroma of sautéed sake lees with oysters is irresistable! The smooth taste makes it a perfect accompaniment to rice.

Serves 2

½ lb (200 g) raw oysters (about 10)
¼ medium onion
½ medium carrot
6 broccoli florets
6 white mushrooms
1 garlic clove
2 tablespoons vegetable oil
¼ cup (50 g) Sake Lees Paste (see page 75)
1¼ cups (300 ml) water
¾ cup (200 ml) unsweetened soy milk
2 to 3 tablespoons cornstarch or potato starch, plus more for dusting the oysters
Salt and pepper, to taste
Rice and chopped parsley, to serve

1 Cut the onion into wedges. Cut the carrot into ¼-inch (5-mm) rounds. Slice the garlic clove thinly, and the mushrooms thickly. Dust the oysters with cornstarch, wash well and drain into a colander. Pat dry and coat with 2 to 3 tablespoons cornstarch.

2 Heat the oil and garlic in a pan over medium-low heat. Add the oysters and cook until lightly browned on both sides. Take out the oysters.

3 Put the onion, carrot and mushrooms in the pan and sauté quickly. Add the water, bring to a boil and skim the surface. Dissolve the Sake Lees Paste with some of the liquid from the pan in a small bowl and add it to the pan. Cover the pan with a lid and simmer until the carrot is tender, about 10 minutes.

4 Add the soy milk and sautéed oysters and bring to a boil. Season to taste with salt and pepper. Add the broccoli florets and heat until cooked through. Serve with rice and scatter with chopped parsley.

Bell Peppers Marinated in Ume Vinegar

Serves 2

½ red and ½ yellow bell pepper
2 teaspoons ume plum vinegar (available in Asian grocery stores)
1 teaspoon (5 g) amazake, concentrated type (see page 11 for a homemade recipe)

Deseed and slice the bell peppers into bite-sized pieces. Place all the ingredients into a plastic bag, knead lightly, and leave for at least 15 minutes to marinate.

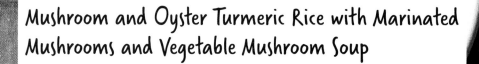

Mushroom and Oyster Turmeric Rice with Marinated Mushrooms and Vegetable Mushroom Soup

Greens with Marinated Mushrooms ➡ Page 81

Mushroom Vegetable Soup ➡ Page 81

Mushroom and Oyster Turmeric Rice ➡ Page 80

This is a colorful rice dish reminiscent of paella or pilaf. Pair it with a mushroom- and vegetable-rich side dish and soup. The addition of turmeric makes this Japanese-inspired fare the perfect fusion food.

Mushrooms Marinated in Shio Koji

By simply mixing boiled mushrooms and shio koji, you can make a stock item that is very useful when you don't know what to make for dinner. You can mix this with pasta or vegetables—it goes with anything.

Shelf life: 1 WEEK IN THE REFRIGERATOR

10 oz (300 g) mixed mushrooms of your choice (such as shiitake, enoki, maitake)
3 tablespoons (60 g) Homemade Shio Koji (see page 9 for a homemade recipe)
2 cups (500 ml) water

NOTE Boil the mushrooms and reserve the boiling liquid. You can use that to make a delicious soup. Or just add water to the marinated mushrooms and heat it to make a soup.

Instructions

1 Put the water in a small pan and bring to a boil over high heat. Add the mushrooms and hold them down in the water with chopsticks or a wooden spoon.

2 Once the water is bubbling, cook for 2 minutes while skimming the surface.

3 Drain into a colander, and leave for at least 15 minutes. (Reserve the cooking liquid to use for the soup.)

4 Mix the mushrooms together with the shio koji and transfer to a preserving jar.

Uses for Shio Koji Marinated Mushrooms

➡ **DELICIOUS AS IS**
Eat the marinated mushrooms drizzled with sesame oil or as a refreshing side dish with grated daikon.

➡ **WITH TOMATOES AS A QUICK PASTA SAUCE** Just put olive oil and a can of tomatoes in a frying pan, add the marinated mushrooms and heat through for 2 minutes. This makes a delicious pasta sauce on busy days.

➡ **AS A SOUP BASE**
Put some marinated mushrooms into a small pan with water and bring to a boil to make a delicious soup. Season with soy sauce to impart a Japanese flavor or add a bay leaf and olive oil for a European twist. Or add sesame oil for a Chinese version.

Mushroom and Oyster Turmeric Rice

Cook the rice with the marinated mushrooms cradled on top. If you mix them in, they're liable to burn.

Serves 2

1 cup (150 g) uncooked white rice
4 raw oysters
⅛ medium onion
2 garlic cloves
¾ cup (150 g) Mushrooms Marinated in Shio Koji (see page 79)
¾ cup (200 ml) water
⅛ teaspoon turmeric powder
1 tablespoon olive oil
Minced parsley, to garnish

1 Finely mince the onion and garlic. Wash the oysters in salted water and pat dry. Rinse the rice and drain in a colander.

2 Heat the olive oil, onion and garlic in a pan. When fragrant, add the oysters and quickly pan fry on both sides. Take out the oysters.

3 Add the rice, sauté until transparent, then add the water and turmeric and increase the heat to high. Bring to a boil, top with the marinated mushrooms and oysters, cover and cook over low heat for 12 minutes. Turn off the heat, steam for 15 minutes, serve and sprinkle with parsley.

Mushroom Vegetable Soup

Serves 2

½ lb (200 g) combined onion, carrot, daikon radish and bell pepper
Reserved cooking liquid from Mushrooms Marinated in Shio Koji recipe (see page 79)
Scant ½ cup (100 ml) water
One 2-inch (5-cm) square piece of dried kombu seaweed
2 tablespoons sake
Salt and pepper, to taste

1 Cut all the vegetables into small ¼-inch (5-mm) dice.
2 Bring the mushroom cooking liquid to a boil in a small pan. Add the water and turn the heat up to high. Skim the surface.
3 Add the vegetables and kombu seaweed and heat through. Season with salt and pepper.

NOTE If you do not have any reserved mushroom cooking liquid simply use ½ cup (100 g) of Mushrooms Marinated in Shio Koji (see page 79) and add it to 2 cups (500 ml) water.

Greens with Marinated Mushrooms

Serves 2

6 oz (150 g) or one bunch leafy greens such as spinach, bok choy or mustard greens
1 cup (200 g) Mushrooms Marinated in Shio Koji (see page 79)
Rice vinegar, to taste

1 Blanch the greens, about 1 minute, then drain and immerse in cold water. Drain again and squeeze out tightly. Cut into easy-to-eat pieces. Finely mince the marinated mushrooms.
2 Arrange the greens on a serving plate, top with the marinated mushrooms and drizzle with a little rice vinegar.

Stir-Fried Pickled Greens with Millet Rice, Natto and Mackerel and Daikon Sake Lees Soup

Stir-Fried Pickled Greens ➡ Page 85

Natto

Glutinous Millet Rice ➡ Page 69

Mackerel and Daikon Sake Lees Soup ➡ Page 85

This meal is made with pickled greens that are in season in the colder months. The miso soup with sake lees and the natto on the side detoxify the body as only fermented foods can.

Salted Pickled Greens

Make use of greens that are in season when they're at their tasty best. You can also enjoy mature pickled greens like traditional Japanese pickled takana and nozawana greens. The longer you pickle the greens, the more sour they'll become, little by little.

Shelf life: 3 WEEKS IN THE REFRIGERATOR

1 lb 2 oz (500 g) baby bokchoy, about 4 heads (or 1 bunch mustard greens)
1 tablespoon sea salt
One 2-inch (5-cm) square piece dried kombu seaweed
1 red chili pepper, deseeded

1 Wash the baby bokchoy well. Slice the stems lengthwise to split each one in half. Dry for 2 to 3 hours (or up to half a day), until they're a little wilted.
2 Rub the salt into the bokchoy so that it's evenly distributed on the leaves (rub more into the stem ends). Leave until the salt dissolves and the greens are wilted, about an hour.
3 Knead the greens lightly with your hands (reserve the water that's released) and pack into a preserving container tightly leaving no gaps. Insert the kombu seaweed pieces and red chili pepper in between the greens. Put a piece of cling wrap right on top of the greens and press down hard.
4 Place a weight on top of the greens (one that weighs twice the weight of the greens) and leave for about half a day. When water comes out of the greens, remove the weight, cover the container with a lid and put into the vegetable compartment of the refrigerator. They can be eaten as lightly pickled greens in 2 to 3 days.

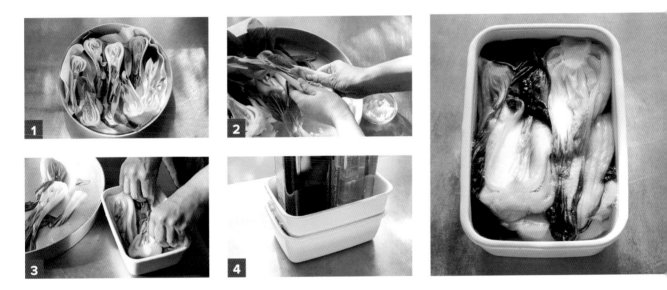

Uses for Salted Pickled Greens

➡ DELICIOUS EATEN AS IS
Cut up the pickled greens and serve topped with katsuobushi (skipjack tuna or bonito flakes) or sesame seeds. This is an easy dish you can make without cooking.

➡ USE IN FRIED RICE
Mince the pickled greens finely and stir-fry with sesame oil and rice. This makes an irresistably delicious fried rice.

➡ MIX WITH NATTO
Instead of the usual minced green onion, try using minced pickled greens mixed into natto. You won't be able to stop eating rice with it!

Stir-Fried Pickled Greens

Pickled greens are great with rice, in ramen noodles or as a side dish for somen.

Serves 2

¾ cup (100 g) mature pickled greens (ones that have turned sour)
1 tablespoon sesame oil
½ garlic clove, finely minced
½ red chili or jalapeno pepper, sliced into rounds
Soy sauce, to taste
Mirin, to taste
½ tablespoon roasted sesame seeds

1 Chop the pickled greens finely. Immerse in water briefly, drain and squeeze out the excess water.
2 Heat the sesame oil, garlic and chili pepper in a frying pan over low heat and stir-fry. When it's fragrant, add the pickled greens and stir-fry briefly.
3 Season to taste with soy sauce and mirin. Add the sesame seeds and mix quickly.

NOTE This is also delicious with some finely powdered katsuobushi dried tuna flakes sprinkled on top.

Mackerel and Daikon Sake Lees Soup (Kasujiru)

Serves 2

1¼ cups (150 g) daikon radish
½ medium carrot
1 teaspoon sesame oil
6 oz (180 g) canned mackerel or sardines in water
½ cup (100 g) Sake Lees Paste (see page 75)
1⅔ cups (400 ml) water
Grated ginger, to garnish

1 Cut the daikon radish and carrot into quarters lengthwise, and slice ¼ inch (5 mm) thick.
2 Put the vegetables and sesame oil into a small pan and sauté quickly. Add the canned mackerel, liquid and all, and add the sake lees paste.
3 Add the water and bring to a boil. Skim the surface and oil that comes to the surface, cover the pan and simmer over low heat for 10 minutes. Serve topped with some grated ginger.

Panfried Swordfish with Spicy Miso, Cucumber Salad, Okra Miso Soup and Barley Rice

Panfried Swordfish with Lettuce Leaves and Spicy Miso ➡ Page 88

Cucumber Salad ➡ Page 89

Spicy Miso Sauce

Barley Rice ➡ Page 88

Spicy Okra Miso Soup ➡ Page 89

Lightly panfried fish is served with a spicy sauce made from miso and amazake. All of these dishes can be made in 5 to 10 minutes, so why not add them to your regular rotation?

Spicy Miso Sauce

This is a delicious and easy sauce to make that is brimming with umami flavors. It keeps well and as time passes, this spicy concoction becomes richer in flavor and even more delicious!

Shelf life: 3 WEEKS IN THE REFRIGERATOR

- ⅓ cup (100 g) Homemade Brown Rice Miso (see page 13 for a homemade recipe)
- 3 tablespoons (50 g) Homemade Amazake Gochujang (see page 65 for a homemade recipe) or regular gochujang
- ½ cup (100 g) amazake, concentrated type (see page 11 for a homemade recipe)
- 2 tablespoons sesame oil
- 1 tablespoon ground sesame
- ½ garlic clove, crushed

Instructions

1 Put all the ingredients in a bowl.

2 Mix well, and transfer to a preserving container.

Uses for Spicy Miso Sauce

➡ **TO FLAVOR MEAT OR FISH**
This miso, less spicy than gochujang, is similar to Korean yangnyeom sauce, so it's delicious rubbed onto meat or fish.

➡ **AS A RAW VEGETABLE DIP**
If you dip chilled cabbage or cucumber in this sauce, you won't be able to stop eating it. It's also great on hand-rolled sushi.

➡ **GREAT FOR BARBECUES**
Ideal for grilled shrimp, oysters and other seafood or grilled shiitake mushrooms and vegetables. It's perfect on grilled eggplant.

Panfried Swordfish with Lettuce Leaves and Spicy Miso

Serves 4

1 lb (450 g) swordfish fillets
1 teaspoon sea salt
2 teaspoons sesame oil
4–8 lettuce leaves
Green shiso or perilla leaves
   (optional)
Thinly sliced onion, to taste
Spicy Miso Sauce (see page 87), to
   serve

1 Sprinkle the fish with a little salt and let stand for 10 minutes. Wipe off the moisture with a paper towel and cut into bite-sized chunks.
2 Heat the sesame oil in a frying pan, add the fish and panfry over medium-low heat until browned on both sides. Serve with the vegetables. Wrap a chunk of the fish in a leaf with a dab of the Spicy Miso Sauce.

Barley Rice

Serves 2

1 cup (150 g) uncooked white rice
1 cup (240 ml) water plus more for
   soaking the barley
2 tablespoons pressed or rolled
   barley

1 Rinse the rice and place in a pot with the water. Put the barley in a small bowl and cover with plenty of water. Leave both to soak for at least 30 minutes.
2 Drain the barley well and add to the rice with a pinch of salt. Mix once, cover the pan and heat over high until the water comes to a boil. Turn the heat down as low as possible, and cook for 15 minutes. Raise the heat to high again for a few seconds until you hear crackling sounds coming from the pan.

Take the pan off the heat and leave the rice to steam and rest for 15 minutes.

Cucumber Salad

Serves 2

1 baby cucumber or 2 pickling gherkins
½ teaspoon sea salt
½ teaspoon lemon juice
1 teaspoon sesame oil
Ground sesame seeds, to taste

1 Sprinkle the cucumber with salt and roll it several times on a cutting board. Cut the cucumber in half lengthwise, and slice thinly.
2 Put the sliced cucumber in a bowl and mix with the lemon juice and sesame oil. Season to taste with salt, and sprinkle with the sesame seeds.

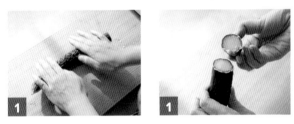

Spicy Okra Miso Soup

Serves 2

1 cup (100 g) okra
1⅔ cups (400 ml) kombu seaweed water (see page 35)
2 teaspoons Spicy Miso Sauce (see page 87)
Soy sauce, to taste

1 Slice the okra.
2 Put the kombu seaweed water and Spicy Miso Sauce in a small pan over medium heat. When it comes a boil, skim the surface, add the okra and turn off the heat. Season to taste with soy sauce.

Mackerel Simmered in Sake with Pickled Greens, Sweet Potato Rice and Root Vegetable Soy Milk Miso Soup

Mackerel Simmered in Sake and Fermented Rice Bran

Greens Pickled in Rice Bran

Sweet Potato Rice

Daikon and Carrot Miso Soy Milk Soup

Rice bran is not just for pickling. Cooking fish with sake, mirin, ginger and rice bran pickling base (nuka miso) gives it a very refreshing taste.

Greens Pickled in Rice Bran

Serves 2

¾ lb (350 g) mustard greens or Swiss chard
½ red chili pepper, sliced into rounds
1 cup (200 g) rice bran pickling base (see page 33)
Sesame oil, to drizzle

1 Cut the tough root ends off the greens and cut the stems in half lengthwise.
2 Put the greens, chili pepper and rice bran pickling base in a plastic bag. Knead the bag lightly to blend the ingredients. Push out the air from the bag, close it up tightly and leave it for about half a day.
3 Rinse off the rice bran pickling base, squeeze out the excess water and slice into serving pieces. Serve drizzled with sesame oil.

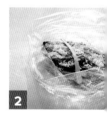

Mackerel Simmered in Sake and Fermented Rice Bran

Serves 4

1 lb (450 g) fresh mackerel, sardines or bluefin fillets
2 to 3 tablespoons soy sauce
4 tablespoons mirin
4 tablespoons sake
1-in (2-cm) piece ginger, thinly sliced
1 cup (225 ml) water
2 tablespoons (35 g) fermented rice bran base (page 33)

NOTE Turn off the heat and let the fish cool down so it absorbs the flavors of the broth. It's also delicious if made in advance and refrigerated.

1 Wash the fish and make slits on the skin sides.
2 Put the soy sauce, mirin, sake, ginger and water in a pan and bring to a boil. Add the fish, skin side down.
3 When it comes back to a boil, turn the heat down to low, skim the surface and then cover with a piece of crumpled kitchen parchment paper. Simmer for 10 minutes.
4 Add the fermented rice bran base, spoon the sauce over the fish, and simmer for an additional 10 minutes or so.

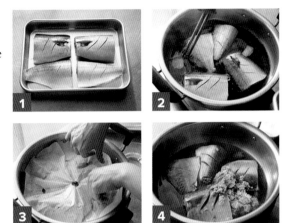

Daikon and Carrot Miso Soy Milk Soup

Serves 2

½ lb (200 g) combined daikon and carrot
2 tablespoons (35 g) white miso (see page 15 for a homemade recipe)
1⅔ cups (400 ml) kombu seaweed water (see page 35)
3½ tablespoons soy milk
Sea salt, to taste
2 teaspoons vegetable oil

Substitution: **Try the same amount of Sake Lees Paste (see page 75) instead of the white miso.**

1 Cut the daikon radish and carrot into sticks.
2 Heat the vegetables and the oil in a small pan over low heat and sauté quickly. Add the kombu seaweed water and bring to a boil. Skim the surface and simmer until the vegetables are tender.
3 Dissolve the white miso in the soy milk in a small bowl and add to the pan. Take the pan off the heat just before it comes back to a boil. Season to taste with salt.

Sweet Potato Rice

Serves 2

1 cup (150 g) uncooked white rice
1 cup (240 ml) water
½ cup (100 g) sweet potato
½ tablespoon sake
½ teaspoon sea salt
½ piece dried kombu seaweed
Roasted sesame seeds, to taste

1 Rinse the rice and place in a pot with the water. Cut the sweet potato into ½-inch (1-cm) dice and soak in a bowl of water for at least 15 minutes. Drain.
2 Put the rice, sweet potato, sake, salt and kombu seaweed in a pan. Mix once, cover the pan and heat on high until the water comes to a boil. Turn the heat down as low as possible, and cook for 15 minutes. Raise the heat to high again for a few seconds until you hear crackling sounds coming from the pan. Take the pan off the heat and let the rice steam and rest for 15 minutes. Serve sprinkled with sesame seeds.

Tempeh Teriyaki with Brown Rice and Umeboshi Seaweed Soup

Tempeh Teriyaki ➡ Page 94

Brown rice

Umeboshi and Kombu
Seaweed Soup ➡ Page 95

Have you ever tried tempeh? It's a mild-flavored fermented meat subtitute
made from soybeans. When served in a sweet and spicy teriyaki sauce,
it's sure to make you want to pile on the rice!

Homemade Fermented Mayonnaise

This is a homemade mayonnaise made without eggs that has a deep, rich flavor. Amazake and ume vinegar are the keys to its flavor.

Shelf life: 2 WEEKS IN THE REFRIGERATOR

2 tablespoons (35 g) amazake, concentrated type (see page 11 for a homemade recipe)
1½ tablespoons soy milk
1½ tablespoons ume vinegar
½ teaspoon sea salt
Scant ½ cup (100 ml) vegetable oil

Uses for Homemade Fermented Mayonnaise

➡ IN SANDWICHES
Mix this mayonnaise with canned tuna for delicious sandwiches stuffed with sliced cucumber.

➡ SHRIMP WITH MAYONNAISE
Mix the mayonnaise with Homemade Amazake Gochujang (see page 65), and add boiled shrimp to make a classic Japanese-Chinese dish: shrimp with mayonnaise.

➡ TARTAR SAUCE
Mix the mayonnaise with finely chopped Homemade Mirin Pickles (see page 47) of your choice. It becomes a great tartar sauce to serve with fried foods.

Instructions

Put the amazake and the soy milk in a bowl and mix together quickly with a spatula. Add the ume vinegar and immediately process in a blender.

Add the oil little by little and continue blending.

When it thickens, add the rest of the oil and blend again.

It's done when it's emulsified and very thick like this.

Tempeh Teriyaki

Cut the tempeh into large pieces to make it more appetizing. If you cook it until it is crispy, the sweet-salty sauce will caramelize and coat it well.

Serves 2

½ lb (200 g) tempeh
4 tablespoons mirin
1⅓ tablespoons soy sauce
1 tablespoon cornstarch or
   rice flour
Vegetable oil, for frying
Accompaniments: lettuce,
   blanched green beans, cherry
   tomatoes, cucumber and
   avocado
Homemade Fermented Mayonaise,
   to serve (see page 93)

1 Cut the tempeh into bite-sized pieces. Wet the surface lightly with water and sprinkle with cornstarch or rice flour.
2 Heat up the oil in a frying pan. Add the tempeh, fry on both sides and remove.
3 Put the mirin in the pan and heat over medium. When it comes to a boil, turn the heat down to low and cook until it has thickened. Add the soy sauce, return the tempeh to the pan and coat the pieces with the sauce.
4 Slice the Accompaniments and arrange them on a platter. Serve with the Accompaniments and Homemade Fermented Mayonnaise.

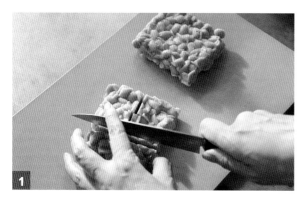

NOTE If you cook down the mirin, the sauce will become thick and nutty.

Umeboshi and Kombu Seaweed Soup

The salty, tangy preserved fruit pairs perfectly with the kombu in this simple yet deeply satisfying soup. Give it a try!

Serves 1

1 umeboshi (salted preserved Japanese plums)
2-in (5-cm) square dried kombu seaweed
⅔ to 1 cup (150 to 225 ml) boiling water
Soy sauce, to taste

Put the umeboshi in a soup bowl and break it up. Add the kombu seaweed and the water and season to taste with a few drops of soy sauce.

Tofu Cheese Salad with Creamy Kabocha Soy Milk Soup

Tofu Cheese Salad

Creamy Kabocha Soy Milk Soup

This preparation is a bit of a surprise, giving the tofu a cheese-like flavor and texture. The creamy kabocha soup, enhanced with shio koji, offers the perfect warming counterpoint.

Tofu Cheese Salad

Serves 2

2 pieces Shio Koji Tofu Cheese
  (⅓ pound/5 oz), see facing page
½ avocado
6–8 cherry tomatoes
½ medium apple
6 lettuce leaves
¼ small red onion
4–6 black olives
½ lemon
1 tablespoon olive oil
Ground black pepper, to taste
Dried oregano, to taste
Bread of your choice

1 Cut the tofu cheese into ½-inch (1-cm) dice. (You can wipe off the shio koji or leave it on.) Dice the fruit and vegetables. Rip up the lettuce with your hands if using larger leaves. Slice the red onion thinly, put it into a bowl of water, then drain.
2 Line the serving plates with lettuce, and top with the vegetables, fruit and tofu cheese. Drizzle with olive oil, sprinkle with oregano and pepper, and serve with bread.

Shio Koji Tofu Cheese

When tofu is marinated in shio koji, it tastes like feta. It is also delicious eaten Japanese style with katsuobushi (skipjack tuna bonito flakes), sesame oil and soy sauce.

Shelf life: 1 WEEK IN THE REFRIGERATOR

1 block firm tofu (10 oz/300 g)
4 tablespoons (80 g) Homemade Shio Koji (see page 9 for a homemade recipe—You can also substitute 8 tablespoons of sake lees for the shio koji.

1 Line a container with cling wrap and place the tofu on top.
2 Put a weight on the tofu and refrigerate overnight.
3 Drain off the water, put a heavier weight on the tofu, and refrigerate it again. Drain off the water again.
4 Cut the tofu into four pieces, place each piece on a sheet of cling wrap, spread 1 tablespoon of shio koji on top and wrap it up. Leave to marinate in the container. It can be eaten the next day or leave it for 2 to 3 days for a deeper flavor.

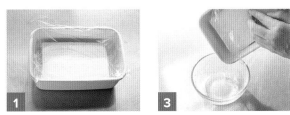

Creamy Kabocha Soy Milk Soup

Serves 2

¼ kabocha or butternut squash (7 oz/200 g), peeled, cleaned and deseeded
1 tablespoon vegetable oil
½ medium onion
1¼ cups (300 ml) water
1 tablespoon (20 g) Homemade Shio Koji (see page 9 for a homemade recipe)
Scant ½ cup (100 ml) soy milk
Salt and pepper, to taste

NOTE You can use the shio koji that's removed from the tofu cheese for the soup.

1 Peel the squash and cut it into small pieces. Slice the onion thinly against the grain.
2 Heat the oil, squash and onion in a pan over medium heat and sauté until the onion is translucent. Add the water, bring to a boil and skim the surface. Turn the heat down to low, cover the pan with a lid and simmer for about 20 minutes.
3 Mash the squash with a spatula, add the shio koji and bring back to a boil. Add the soy milk to thin out the soup, and then heat until just before coming to a boil. Season to taste with salt and pepper.

Shio Koji Potatoes Gratin with Vegetable Lentil Soup and Quick Pickles

Red Cabbage and Radish Quick Pickles ➡ Page 101

Shio Koji Potatoes Gratin ➡ Page 100

Lentil and Napa Cabbage Shio Koji Tomato Soup ➡ Page 101

The star of this meal is a baked gratin that can be made without butter, milk, cheese or cream. The lentil tomato soup provides plenty of protein and minerals with its range of vegetables.

Shio Koji White Sauce

The creamy shio koji produces a smooth and rich white sauce similar to bechamel but without any dairy products. Use coconut oil (the unscented type) to give it an unctuous, buttery flavor.

Serves 4
Shelf life: 4 TO 5 DAYS IN THE REFRIGERATOR

2 tablespoons rice flour
4 tablespoons vegetable oil (such as coconut oil)
½ garlic clove, crushed
2 cups plus 1 tablespoon (500 ml) unsweetened soy milk
2 tablespoons (40 g) Homemade Shio Koji (see page 9 for a homemade recipe)
White pepper, to taste

You can substitute 2 tablespoons of sake lees paste and ⅓ teaspoon sea salt for the shio koji.

Instructions

1 Put the rice flour and oil in a pan, and mix together until smooth.

2 Turn the heat to low, heat for about 1 minute until small bubbles form, add the garlic and mix in then turn off the heat. Wait for the bubbles to disappear (this gets rid of the garlic odor).

3 When the garlic odor is gone, add the soy milk little by little while mixing with a whisk. Add the shio koji and mix again.

4 Heat over medium heat. When it starts to bubble, turn the heat down to low and simmer for another 2 minutes while stirring. Season with white pepper.

Uses for Shio Koji White Sauce

➡ **FOR CLAM CHOWDER**
Thin out the white sauce with soy milk, then add boiled potatoes and shelled clams.

➡ **ON VEGETABLES AS A CREAM SAUCE** Just sauté cabbage, turnips or napa cabbage, add some white sauce and simmer briefly. The umami of the shio koji will make you want to spoon this dish over rice.

Shio Koji Potatoes Gratin

Instead of cheese and butter, a white sauce made with shio koji gives this dish a fabulous flavor.

Serves 2

2 potatoes (½ lb/200 g), peeled and cut into slices of about ⅛ in (3 mm) thick
1 small king oyster mushroom, sliced
2 salted canned anchovies (optional)
¾ cup (200 g) Shio Koji White Sauce
Olive oil, to drizzle
Ground black pepper, to taste

NOTE This is also delicious sprinkled with breadcrumbs or cheese.

Instructions

Preheat the oven to 390°F (200°C). Peel and slice the potatoes. Spread the inside of two ovenproof gratin dishes thinly with olive oil. Add the sliced potato and mushroom. Rip up the anchovies and distribute the pieces on the potato evenly.

Pour in the white sauce, drizzle the surface with olive oil, and bake in a 390°F (200°C) oven until the edges are browned for about 30 minutes. Sprinkle with pepper and serve.

Red Cabbage and Radish Quick Pickles

Serves 2

4 radishes
1 large red cabbage leaf
1 cup (200 g) rice bran pickling base (see page 33)
Sea salt, to taste

1 Rub salt into the cabbage and the radishes and let stand for at least an hour.
2 When the moisture has been released, pat them dry. Put the vegetables into the rice bran pickling base for about 3 hours. Remove and cut into easy-to-eat pieces.

NOTES
• Quickly pickled rice bran pickles can be eaten like salad.
• If they're too salty, soak them in water for a while, then squeeze them out.
• The vegetables are delicious drizzled with a little olive oil too.

Lentil and Napa Cabbage Shio Koji Tomato Soup

This is a hearty and satisfying soup that is easy to throw together quickly. The shio koji gives it real depth.

Serves 2

½ medium onion
½ garlic clove
½ cup (30–40 g) carrots and celery
1 large napa cabbage leaf
1 tablespoon vegetable oil
2 tablespoons (40 g) Homemade Shio Koji (see page 9 for a homemade recipe)
½ small can (7 oz/200 g) diced tomatoes
1¼ cups (300 ml) water
¼ cup (50 g) cooked lentils
Boiled broccoli florets (optional)

1 Finely mince the onion, garlic, carrot and celery. Cut the napa cabbage into ½-inch (1-cm) dice. Rinse the lentils and drain.
2 Heat the oil and garlic in a pan over low heat. When it's fragrant, add the other vegetables and sauté quickly. Add the shio koji and mix it in.
3 Add the canned tomatoes, water and lentils. When it comes to a boil, simmer for about 10 minutes, then turn off the heat. Season to taste with salt. Optionally add some boiled broccoli.

Salmon and Napa Cabbage Hot Pot with Fermented Aromatic Chili Oil

Fermented Aromatic Chili Oil

Salmon and Napa Cabbage Fermented Hot Pot

This hot pot based on soy milk and shio koji is perfect for a cold night. The homemade chili oil is irresistible!

Salmon and Napa Cabbage Hot Pot

Serves 2

2-inch (5-cm) square piece dried kombu seaweed
1¼ cups (300 ml) water
1 thin leek or 2 green onions
2 large napa cabbage leaves
⅓ lb (150 g) komatsuna greens or Swiss chard
2 salmon filets (½ lb/225 g)
½ atsuage thick deep-fried tofu (about 4 oz/120 g)
½ carrot
6 shiitake mushrooms

A INGREDIENTS

1 cup (240 ml) soy milk
2 tablespoons sesame paste or tahini
2 tablespoons (40 g) Homemade Shio Koji (see page 9 for a homemade recipe)

Fermented Aromatic Chili Oil, to serve (see below)
Minced green onions, to serve

You can substitute 2 tablespoons sake lees plus ⅓ teaspoon sea salt for the shio koji.

1 Put the kombu seaweed and water in a pan. Slice the green onion or leek diagonally. Cut the greens and napa cabbage into 1-inch (2- to 3-cm) pieces. Cut up the salmon, atsuage, carrot and shiitake mushrooms into easy-to-eat pieces.

2 Mix the **A** ingredients together well, add them to the pan and bring to a boil. Add all the ingredients except for the greens and simmer over medium-low heat for 6 to 7 minutes. Add the greens at the end, bring back to a boil, then turn off the heat. Serve with Fermented Aromatic Chili Oil and minced green onions.

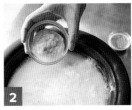

NOTE This hot pot is also delicious if you add udon noodles.

Fermented Aromatic Chili Oil

This chili oil is done in just 5 minutes of cooking. I recommend putting it on tofu or somen noodles too.

Serves 2
Shelf life: 2 WEEKS IN THE REFRIGERATOR

¼ medium onion
2 garlic cloves
1 teaspoon minced ginger
¼ lotus root (2 oz/50 g)

A INGREDIENTS

1 teaspoon coarsely ground red pepper
⅓ teaspoon sansho pepper
6½ tablespoons vegetable oil
4 tablespoons (80 g) Homemade Shio Koji (see page 9 for a homemade recipe)
2 tablespoons roasted sesame seeds

You can substitute 4 tablespoons sake lees plus ⅔ teaspoon sea salt for the shio koji.

1 Finely mince the onion, garlic, and ginger. Roughly mince the lotus root.

2 Put the Step 1 ingredients and the **A** ingredients in a frying pan, mix well, and turn the heat on to medium.

3 When the mixture starts to bubble turn the heat down to low, heat for about 5 minutes and then take off the heat.

4 Add the shio koji and the sesame seeds and mix. Transfer to a preserving container.

NOTE If you want to make it spicier, add more chili.

Recipe Index by Ingredient

Search for recipes according to the ingredients you have on hand or ones that you like. (Ingredients used in basic seasonings and toppings are not included.)

Fermented Ingredients

Shio Koji
Homemade Shio Koji 9
Fermented Onion Paste 23
Fried Shio Koji Marinated Tuna Nuggets with Asparagus 27
Radish and Sweet Onion Quick Pickled in Shio Koji 27
Mushrooms Marinated in Shio Koji 79
Shio Koji Tofu Cheese 97
Shio Koji White Sauce 99
Shio Koji Potatoes Gratin 100
Lentil and Napa Cabbage Shio Koji Tomato Soup 101
Salmon and Napa Cabbage Hot Pot 103
Fermented Aromatic Chili Oil 103

Amazake
Amazake, Concentrated Type 11
Amazake French Dressing 29
Clams Simmered in Amazake 37
Mackerel and Amazake Curry 39
Amazake Lemon Lassi Drink 39
Homemade Cabbage Amazake Kimchi 45
Amazake Fruit Yogurt 46
Refreshing Plum or Apricot Miso 49
Fragrant Green Chili Miso 53
Eggplant Sautéed in Ume Vinegar 55
Crunchy Dried Daikon Pickled with Amazake 59
Homemade Amazake Gochujang 65
Tofu and Shiitake Mushroom Bibimbap 66
White Leek Soup 66
Four Types of Namul 67
Bell Peppers Marinated in Ume Vinegar 77
Spicy Miso Sauce 87
Homemade Fermented Mayonnaise 93

Brown Rice Miso • Miso
Homemade Brown Rice Miso 13
White Chickpea Miso 15
Sweet Onion and Radish Leaf Miso Soup 27
Refreshing Plum or Apricot Miso 49
Zucchini and Aburaage Miso Soup 51
Fragrant Green Chili Miso 53
Root Vegetable Soup with Brown Rice Miso 69
Diced Vegetables Pickled in Miso 69
Spicy Miso Sauce 87

White Miso
Amazake French Dressing 29
Clam and White Miso Turmeric Soup 29
Sea Bream and Clams Steamed in White Miso and
    Wine 31
White Miso Lemon Dip Crudités 31
Mountain Yam White Miso Soup 35
Spring Vegetable Miso Soup 45
Sake Lees Pickling Base (Kasudoko) 71
Daikon and Carrot Miso Soy Milk Soup 91

Sake Lees
Sake Lees Pickling Base (Kasudoko) 71
Sake Lees Paste 75

Soy Milk Yogurt
Homemade Soy Milk Yogurt 41
Sardine and Soy Milk Yogurt Curry 42
Amazake Fruit Yogurt 46

Natto • Tempeh
Delicious Natto and Green Bean Fritters 34
Green Chili Miso, Spinach and Natto Soba Noodles 54
Tempeh Teriyaki 94

Fresh Rice Bran
Easy Rice Bran Pickles (Nukazuke) 33

Vegetables and Fruits

Onions • Red Onions
Fermented Onion Paste 23
Radish and Sweet Onion Quick Pickled in Shio Koji 27
Sweet Onion and Radish Leaf Miso Soup 27
Clam and White Miso Turmeric Soup 29
Sea Bream and Clams Steamed in White Miso and
    Wine 31
Mackerel and Amazake Curry 39
Sardine and Soy Milk Yogurt Curry 42
Red Cabbage Marinated in Yogurt 43
Spring Vegetable Miso Soup 45
Homemade Mirin Pickles 47
Octopus and Cucumber with Plum Miso 51
Green Chili Miso, Spinach and Natto Soba Noodles 54
Root Vegetable Soup with Brown Rice Miso 69

Creamy Oysters Sautéed in Sake Lees and Soy Milk 76
Mushroom and Oyster Turmeric Rice 80
Mushroom Vegetable Soup 81
Tofu Cheese Salad 96
Creamy Kabocha Soy Milk Soup 97
Lentil and Napa Cabbage Shio Koji Tomato Soup 101
Fermented Aromatic Chili Oil 103

Carrots
Four Types of Namul 67
Root Vegetable Soup with Brown Rice Miso 69
Diced Vegetables Pickled in Miso 69
Vegetables Pickled in Sake Lees 73
Creamy Oysters Sautéed in Sake Lees and Soy Milk 76
Mushroom Vegetable Soup 81
Mackerel and Daikon Sake Lees Soup (Kasujiru) 85
Daikon Radish and Carrot Miso Soy Milk Soup 91
Lentil and Napa Cabbage Shio Koji Tomato Soup 101
Salmon and Napa Cabbage Hot Pot 103

Potatoes
Fermented Onion Soup 25
Easy Rice Bran Pickles (Nukazuke) 33
Shio Koji Potatoes Gratin 100

Mountain Yam
Mountain Yam White Miso Soup 35

Taro Root
Root Vegetable Soup with Brown Rice Miso 69

Sweet Potatoes
Sweet Potato Rice 91

Kabocha
Creamy Kabocha Soy Milk Soup 97

Lotus Root
Root Vegetable Soup with Brown Rice Miso 69
Fermented Aromatic Chili Oil 103

Daikon • Dried Daikon
Mackerel and Amazake Curry 39
Crunchy Dried Daikon Pickled with Amazake 59
Four Types of Namul 67
Root Vegetable Soup with Brown Rice Miso 69
Diced Vegetables Pickled in Miso 69
Vegetables Pickled in Sake Lees 73
Mushroom Vegetable Soup 81
Daikon Radish and Carrot Miso Soy Milk Soup 91

Leek
White Leek Soup 66
Salmon and Napa Cabbage Hot Pot 103

Burdock Root
Homemade Mirin Pickles 47

Cabbage • Red Cabbage
Red Cabbage Marinated in Yogurt 43
Homemade Cabbage Amazake Kimchi 45
Red Cabbage and Radish Quick Pickles 101

Napa Cabbage
Lentil and Napa Cabbage Shio Koji Tomato Soup 101
Salmon and Napa Cabbage Hot Pot 103

Tomatoes • Cherry Tomatoes
Fermented Onion Soup 25
Sea Bream and Clams Steamed in White Miso and
    Wine 31
Mackerel and Amazake Curry 39
Sardine and Soy Milk Yogurt Curry 42
Tofu Cheese Salad 96

Cucumbers
Octopus and Cucumber with Plum Miso 51
Vegetables Pickled in Sake Lees 73
Cucumber Salad 89

Eggplant
Eggplant Sautéed in Ume Vinegar 55

Okra
Spicy Okra Miso Soup 89

Broccoli
Fermented Onion Soup 25
Hot Salad of Sugar Snap Peas and Broccoli 29
Creamy Oysters Sautéed in Sake Lees and Soy Milk 76

Bell Peppers
Homemade Mirin Pickles 47
Bell Peppers Marinated in Ume Vinegar 77
Mushroom Vegetable Soup 81

Asparagus
Fried Shio Koji Skipjack Tuna and Fried Asparagus 27
Spring Vegetable Miso Soup 45

Sugar Snap Peas
Hot Salad of Sugar Snap Peas and Broccoli 28
Sea Bream and Clams Steamed in White Miso and

Wine 31

Zucchini
Zucchini and Aburaage Miso Soup 51
Sushi Rice with Fermented Ginger and Mixed
    Vegetables 57

Sweet Corn
Sushi Rice with Fermented Ginger and Mixed
    Vegetables 57

Green Beans
Delicious Natto and Green Bean Fritters 34

Soybeans
Sushi Rice with Fermented Ginger and Mixed
    Vegetables 57

Leafy Greens (Spinach, Bokchoy, Komatsuna)
Four Types of Namul 67
Greens with Marinated Mushrooms 81
Salted Pickled Greens 83
Greens Pickled in Rice Bran 90
Salmon and Napa Cabbage Hot Pot 103

Watercress
Clam and White Miso Turmeric Soup 29
Sea Bream and Clams Steamed in White Miso and
    Wine 31
Watercress Rice 31

Broccolini or Nanohana
Clear Soup with Broccolini 61

Mitsuba
Mitsuba Rice 37

Shiso Leaves
Fragrant Green Chili Miso 53

Radishes
Radish and Sweet Onion Quick Pickled in Shio Koji 27
Sweet Onion and Radish Leaf Miso Soup 27
Red Cabbage and Radish Quick Pickles 101

Bean Sprouts
Four Types of Namul 67
Bean Sprout and Sake Lees Soup 73

Garlic
Tender Sautéed Salmon with Fermented Onion
    Sauce 24

Fried Shio Koji Marinated Tuna Nuggets with
    Asparagus 27
Amazake French Dressing 29
Clam and White Miso Turmeric Soup 29
Sea Bream and Clams Steamed in White Miso
    and Wine 31
Mackerel and Amazake Curry 39
Sardine and Soy Milk Yogurt Curry 42
Lemon Rice 43
Homemade Cabbage Amazake Kimchi 45
Homemade Mirin Pickles 47
Eggplant Sautéed in Ume Vinegar 55
Tofu and Shiitake Mushroom Bibimbap 66
Four Types of Namul 67
Bean Sprout and Sake Lees Soup 73
Creamy Oysters Sautéed in Sake Lees and Soy Milk 76
Stir-Fried Pickled Greens 85
Spicy Miso Sauce 87
Shio Koji White Sauce 99
Lentil and Napa Cabbage Shio Koji Tomato Soup 101
Fermented Aromatic Chili Oil 103

Ginger
Fried Shio Koji Marinated Tuna Nuggets with
    Asparagus 27
Delicious Natto and Green Bean Fritters 34
Clams Simmered in Amazake 37
Mackerel and Amazake Curry 39
Sardine and Soy Milk Yogurt Curry 42
Homemade Cabbage Amazake Kimchi 45
Ginger Rice 51
Fermented Myoga Ginger and Regular Ginger 57
Mackerel and Daikon Sake Lees Soup (Kasujiru) 85
Mackerel Simmered in Sake and Fermented Rice
    Bran 91
Fermented Aromatic Chili Oil 103

Myoga Ginger
Fermented Myoga Ginger and Regular Ginger 57

Mushrooms
Homemade Mirin Pickles 47
Tofu and Shiitake Mushroom Bibimbap 66
Creamy Oysters Sautéed in Sake Lees and Soy Milk 76
Mushrooms Marinated in Shio Koji 79
Shio Koji Potatoes Gratin 100
Salmon and Napa Cabbage Hot Pot 103

Lemon • Lemon Juice
Fermented Onion Salad Dressing 25
White Miso Lemon Dip Crudités 31
Amazake Lemon Lassi Drink 39

Lemon Rice 43
Sea Bream and Pickled Daikon Sushi 60
Tofu Cheese Salad 96

Japanese Ume Plums • Umeboshi
Refreshing Plum or Apricot Miso 49
Umeboshi and Kombu Seaweed Soup 95

Fish and Seafood

Tuna
Fried Shio Koji Marinated Tuna Nuggets with
    Asparagus 27
Panfried Fish Marinated in Sake Lees 72

Swordfish
Panfried Swordfish with Lettuce Leaves and
    Spicy Miso 88

Salmon
Tender Sautéed Salmon with Onion 24
Salmon and Napa Cabbage Fermented Hot Pot 103

Sardines
Sardine Soy Milk Yogurt Curry 42

Mackerel
Mackerel Simmered in Sake and Fermented
    Rice Bran 91

Sea Bream
Sea Bream and Clams Steamed in White Miso and
    Wine 31
Sea Bream and Pickled Daikon Sushi 60

Shirasu • Chirimenjako (Salted Whitebait)
Kimchi and Tofu Rice Bowl 45
Sushi Rice with Fermented Ginger and Mixed
    Vegetables 57

Octopus
Octopus and Cucumber with Plum Miso 51

Oysters
Creamy Oysters Sautéed in Sake Lees and Soy Milk 76
Mushroom and Oyster Turmeric Rice 80

Clams
Clam and White Miso Turmeric Soup 29
Sea Bream and Clams Steamed in White Miso
    and Wine 31

Clams Simmered in Amazake 37

Wakame Seaweed
Octopus and Cucumber with Plum Miso 51

Canned Mackerel
Mackerel and Amazake Curry 39
Mackerel and Daikon Sake Lees Soup (Kasujiru) 85

Processed Foods and Dried Foods

Tofu
Clam Stock with Tofu 36
Kimchi Topped Rice 45
Tofu Topped with Fermented Ginger 57
Tofu and Shiitake Mushroom Bibimbap 66
Shio Koji Tofu Cheese 97

**Fried Tofu (Aburaage Thin Fried Tofu and Atsuage
    Thick Fried Tofu**
Zucchini and Aburaage Miso Soup 51
Root Vegetable Soup with Brown Rice Miso 69
Salmon and Napa Cabbage Fermented Hot Pot 103

Soy Milk
Clam and White Miso Turmeric Soup 29
Amazake Lemon Lassi Drink 39
Homemade Soy Milk Yogurt 41
White Leek Soup 66
Daikon and Carrot Miso Soy Milk Soup 91
Homemade Fermented Mayonnaise 93
Shio Koji White Sauce 99
Salmon and Napa Cabbage Hot Pot 103

Various Kinds of Rice and Grains
Rice with Black Sesame Salt 26
Mixed Grain Rice 29
Watercress Rice 31
Mixed "Black" Rice 35
Mitsuba Rice 37
Lemon Rice 43
Kimchi and Tofu Rice Bowl 45
Ginger Rice 51
Sushi Rice with Fermented Ginger and Mixed
    Vegetables 57
Sea Bream and Pickled Daikon Sushi 60
Glutinous Millet Rice 69
Mushroom and Oyster Turmeric Rice 80
Barley Rice 88
Sweet Potato Rice 91

Your Fermentation Pantry

Here are things you can buy in a good Asian food market (or you can order them online). Please note also the recipes are given in this book for making your own amazake and miso at home.

Fermented Food Products

Dried rice koji

Dried brown rice koji

Brown rice miso

Brown rice amazake

White rice amazake

White miso

Sake lees

Chickpea miso

Soy Sauce Products

Whole soybean soy sauce

Barrel-aged soy sauce

Ishiri fish/squid sauce

Soy Bean Products & Chickpeas

Chickpeas

Soy milk yogurt starter

Tempeh starter culture

Natto

Silken tofu

Unsweetened soy milk

Sake, Mirin and Vinegar Products

Cooking sake

Mirin

Ume vinegar, white & red

Oil Products

Extra-virgin olive oil

First-press

Canola oil

Sesame oil

Seaweed and Seafood Products

Kombu seaweed

**Katsuobushi
(skipjack tuna flakes)**

Mackerel, canned

Fermented Foods Are All You Need!

More energy, better gut health and a diet fueled by superfoods, what could be better?

It's not hard to sell people on the many health benefits of fermented foods. Now that you see how easy they are to prepare at home, how simple it is to integrate them into a range of delicious entrees, side dishes and starters, what are you waiting for? Don't let the fermentation revolution continue without you!

Using these time-tested techniques, harnessing the power of the oldest form of food preservation couldn't be easier. These flexible ferments are the building blocks for a diet as delicious as it is healthy.

A final word of thanks: Mr. Aoki, the photographer, and Ms. Nakazato, the stylist, created an array of visually stunning arrangements for this book. The designer, Mr. Fujita, and Mr. Wada, the editor, brought a new level of clarity and understanding to my recipes and advice. And special thanks to Ms. Koshikawa, the editor of the magazine *Croissant*, who has guided me for seven years, starting with a series of articles on fermented meals. I've been following Ms. Koshikawa for a long time. They've all played an important part in my own fermentation journey. I hope yours is as healthful, flavorful and rewarding!

—Hiroko Shirasaki

"Books to Span the East and West"

Tuttle Publishing was founded in 1832 in the small New England town of Rutland, Vermont [USA]. Our core values remain as strong today as they were then—to publish best-in-class books which bring people together one page at a time. In 1948, we established a publishing outpost in Japan—and Tuttle is now a leader in publishing English-language books about the arts, languages and cultures of Asia. The world has become a much smaller place today and Asia's economic and cultural influence has grown. Yet the need for meaningful dialogue and information about this diverse region has never been greater. Over the past seven decades, Tuttle has published thousands of books on subjects ranging from martial arts and paper crafts to language learning and literature—and our talented authors, illustrators, designers and photographers have won many prestigious awards. We welcome you to explore the wealth of information available on Asia at www.tuttlepublishing.com.

Published by Tuttle Publishing, an imprint of Periplus Editions (HK) Ltd.

www.tuttlepublishing.com

SHIRASAKI CHAKAI NO HAKKO TEISHOKU
© Hiroko Shirasaki 2021
English translation rights arranged with
MAGAZINE HOUSE CO., LTD through
Japan UNI Agency, Inc., Tokyo

English Translation ©2023 Periplus Editions (HK) Ltd.

Library of Congress Control Number: 2023934573

ISBN 978-4-8053-1747-1

Printed in China   2305EP
26 25 24 23   10 9 8 7 6 5 4 3 2 1

Distributed by

North America, Latin America & Europe
Tuttle Publishing
364 Innovation Drive
North Clarendon, VT 05759-9436 U.S.A.
Tel: 1 (802) 773-8930; Fax: 1 (802) 773-6993
info@tuttlepublishing.com
www.tuttlepublishing.com

Japan
Tuttle Publishing
Yaekari Building 3rd Floor
5-4-12 Osaki
Shinagawa-ku
Tokyo 141 0032
Tel: (81) 3 5437-0171; Fax: (81) 3 5437-0755
sales@tuttle.co.jp
www.tuttle.co.jp

Asia Pacific
Berkeley Books Pte. Ltd.
3 Kallang Sector, #04-01
Singapore 349278
Tel: (65) 67412178; Fax: (65) 67412179
inquiries@periplus.com.sg
www.tuttlepublishing.com